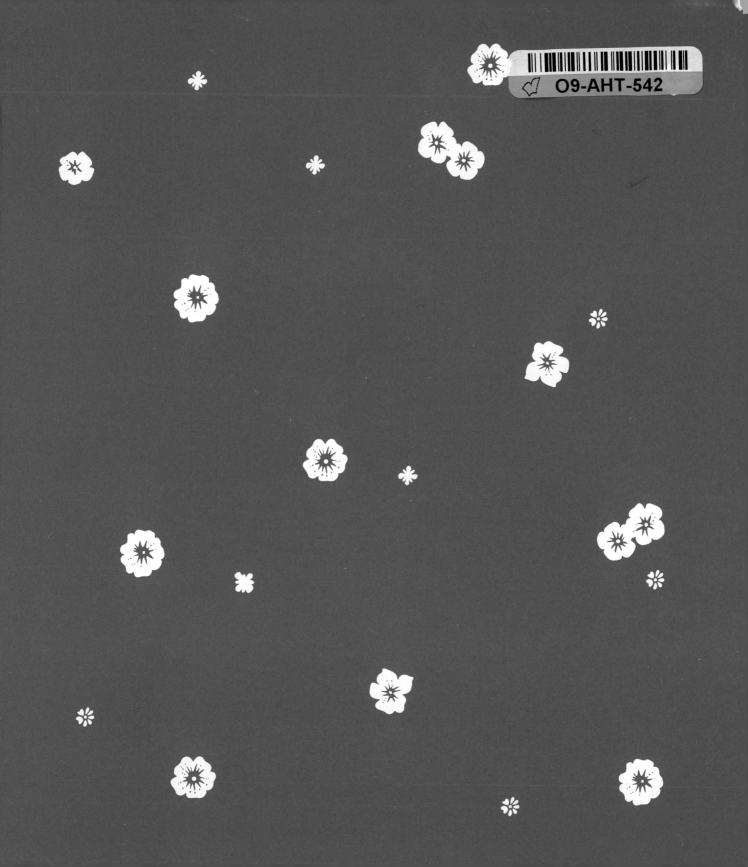

Betty Crocker

Lost Recipes

Beloved Vintage Recipes

for Today's Kitchen

Houghton Mifflin Harcourt
Boston • New York • 2017

GENERAL MILLS

Owned Media and Publishing Director: Amy Halford

Owned Media and Publishing Manager: Danielle Andrews

Senior Editor: Cathy Swanson

Recipe Development and Testing: Betty Crocker Kitchens

Photography: General Mills Photography Studios and Image Library

HOUGHTON MIFFLIN HARCOURT

Editorial Director: Deb Brody

Executive Editor: Anne Ficklen

Managing Editor: Marina Padakis

Production Editor: Helen Seachrist

Cover Design: Tai Blanche

Interior Design and Layout: Tai Blanche

Senior Production Coordinator: Kimberly Kiefer

www.hmhco.com

Library of Congress Cataloging-in-Publication Data is available.

ISBN 978-1-328-71033-8 (hardcover); 978-1-328-71037-6 (ebook)

Manufactured in China

TOP 12

4500841609

Inspiring America to Cook at Home™

The Betty Crocker Kitchens seal guarantees success in your kitchen. Every recipe has been tested in America's Most Trusted Kitchens™ to meet our high standards of reliability, easy preparation and great taste.

FIND MORE GREAT IDEAS AT

BettyCrocker.com

DEAR FRIENDS,

Anadama bread, Welsh Rarebit, Cherry Berries on a Cloud—for some folks, these foods will evoke cherished memories of times past. For many, it will be the introduction to some very special recipes that deserve to come out of recipe boxes again.

Back in their day, food was often saltier and full of fat or very bland, compared to how we eat today. Yeast of yesteryear was different from today's options, so older recipes needed to be updated to be successful now. This special collection of "lost" recipes has been lovingly updated for today's ingredients and tastes. You're going to enjoy serving these to family and friends—when we shot the photos for this book, these foods were devoured!

Try our great get-togethers, sure to make you a party legend. Our festive *Retro Tiki Party*, page 58, will be fun, no matter what the weather. The *Merry Kitschmas Party*, page 25, brings back delicious holiday favorites with a nostalgic twist. *Time for a Tea Party*, page 121, shows a sweet way to entertain kids or your girlfriends.

With each recipe, you'll find the history of the dish or other interesting information. Have a chuckle at the anecdotal quips of wisdom that appeared in the first cookbooks. Since 1921, the Betty Crocker Kitchens have been a trusted source of inspiring-but-doable recipes. That hasn't changed . . . but it's fun to bring back the delicious recipes of where we started.

May all your meals be memorable,

Betty Crocker

CONTENTS

⁓⁓⁓

FEATURES

The History of Food

What's happening around us (and what tickles our taste buds) has transformed our eating choices over the past century. Take a peek at how we've been eating over the past 100 years.

1910s	1920s	1930s	1940s	1950s	1960s
Old-world heritage vs. newly formed unity (aka melting pot) + World War I rationing	Prohibition meets speakeasies; culinary experimentation with foreign foods after soldiers return from the war	Cookbooks suggest shortcuts for cooking, economical recipes and direction for wives to "powder their noses" before serving the meal	Protein-stretching meals, World War II rationing and substitutions	Fill-you-up meals from prepackaged foods and renewed interest in foreign cuisines from returning GIs	Showy French food, soul food and anything you can light on fire

1910s

Old-world heritage vs. newly formed unity (aka melting pot) + World War I rationing

- Lasagna with American cheese

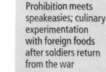

- Chop suey with ground beef
- **How Much?** A loaf of bread cost 3¢

1920s

Prohibition meets speakeasies; culinary experimentation with foreign foods after soldiers return from the war

- Soft drinks were gulped down like never before
- **Betty Crocker Is Born** She is created to reply to cooking- and baking-related questions received from consumers.
- Pineapple upside-down cake

- **A Sign of the Times** Tea sandwiches, chafing-dish recipes

1930s

Cookbooks suggest shortcuts for cooking, economical recipes and direction for wives to "powder their noses" before serving the meal

- **How Much?** A quart of milk cost 14¢

- **1936:** First official portrait of Betty Crocker is released.

- **Cocktails All the Rage** Martini, Old-Fashioned Manhattan, etc.

1940s

Protein-stretching meals, World War II rationing and substitutions

- Mock Apple Pie (crackers replace apples)
- Eggless cakes, sugarless cookies

- Meatless meals and casseroles to make meat go farther

1950s

Fill-you-up meals from prepackaged foods and renewed interest in foreign cuisines from returning GIs

- Betty Crocker's first *Picture Cook Book* introduced

- **Backyard Symbol of American Status** The grill

- Themed dinners popular for entertaining
- **1955:** Betty Crocker or June Cleaver?

1960s

Showy French food, soul food and anything you can light on fire

- **Jacqueline Kennedyish** Betty Crocker circa 1965

- Fondue, Steak Diane and Bananas Foster

100 YEARS of great eating

1970s

All about choices—salad bars are big. Tough times = economical meals

● Hamburger Helper®, granola bars introduced

● **All Business Betty** This 1972 Betty is created to represent the recent significant contributions women are making outside of the home.

● **How Much?** A candy bar cost 15¢

● **The Latest Thing** Slow cookers

1980s

Easy family meals contrast with complicated party foods

● **Updated 'Do** 1980 Betty keeps up with the times.

● Microwave popcorn explodes on to the market.

● Mud pie

1990s

Interest in healthier foods, ready-prepared foods, new and unusual produce

● Beer can chicken

● Bread machines popular as the latest kitchen appliance

● Carambola or "star fruit"

● **1996:** The current image of Betty is a combination of 75 real-life women of diverse backgrounds and ages.

2000s

Ethnic variety as well as familiar comfort foods

● Celebrity chefs and cooking channels

● **Monstrous or Munchkin?** Super-sized or mini versions of everything

● Sushi

2010s

Simplicity, locally grown produce, global cuisine, health-consciousness

● Interest in foods/recipes for health—gluten free, food allergies, low sodium

● Renewed interest in canning

● Sliders, whoopie pies and red velvet cake

● Betty Crocker's all-new 12th edition is introduced in October 2016

● **Birthday Girl** Betty Crocker turns 90! Girl, you REALLY don't age!

WISDOM & TIPS FROM BETTY

Since the very first edition of *The Betty Crocker Cookbook* was published in 1950, Betty has been guiding the women of the day to success, both in and out of the kitchen. Read through these nuggets of wisdom from the first Picture Cook Books for an interesting, and at times amusing, look at the past.

REFRESH YOUR SPIRITS
(*Betty Crocker Picture Cook Book*, 1961)

Every morning before breakfast, comb hair, apply makeup and a dash of cologne. Does wonders for your morale and your family's too!

Think pleasant thoughts while working, and a chore will become a "labor of love."

Have a hobby. Garden, paint pictures, look through magazines for home planning ideas, read a good book or attend club meetings. Be interested and you will always be interesting!

If you have a spare moment, sit down, close your eyes and just relax.

BE COMFORTABLE
(*Betty Crocker Picture Cook Book*, 1961)

Wear comfortable shoes and easy-fitting clothes while working.

Stand erect. Good posture prevents fatigue.

Have sink, work table and counter tops at heights that are comfortable to eliminate strain. If dishpan is too low, set it on a box.

Use a dust mop and long-handled dust pan. Use self-wringing mop to prevent stooping.

MEAL TIME . . . A HAPPY TIME
(*Betty Crocker Picture Cook Book*, 1961)

Make mealtime a special time in your home by serving appetizing food in a relaxed, happy atmosphere. The buoyant health and feeling of well-being that results will be reward enough for the care and loving thought you give to your family's meals.

PLANNING FOODS THAT GO TOGETHER
(*Betty Crocker Picture Cook Book*, 1961)

Something soft and something crisp
Should always go together,
And something hot with something cold
No matter what the weather;
Serve bland foods with tangy sauce
And garnish them with green;
If you will use these simple rules
You'll be your family's queen!

FRESH FRUIT AND CHEESE
(*Betty Crocker Picture Cook Book*, 1961)

The bowl headed with colorful fruit washed, dried and chilled—a variety to choose from . . . is both decorative and tempting. Cheese and crisp unsweetened crackers are natural affinities or crisp rich cookies are pleasant accompaniments. Serving can be very simple: just an individual dessert plate, a suitable knife for cutting fruit and spreading cream cheese. Finger bowls are correct to save linens from stubborn fruit stains but today paper napkins are often used with fruit.

PERFECT YOUR HOMEMAKING SKILLS
(*Betty Crocker Picture Cook Book*, 1950)

Practice each task until it goes smoothly and easily. This develops techniques in meal-planning, cooking, marketing, sewing, dishwashing, home-beautifying, nursing, bed-making, cleaning, laundering.

If you're tired from overwork,
Household chores you're bound to shirk.
Read these pointers tried and true
And discover what to do

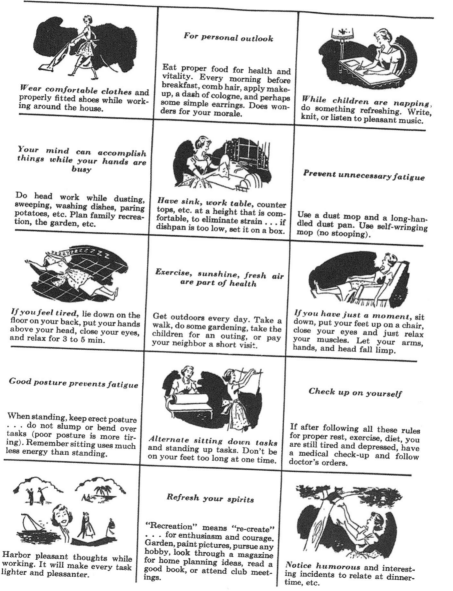

Wear comfortable clothes and properly fitted shoes while working around the house.

For personal outlook

Eat proper food for health and vitality. Every morning before breakfast, comb hair, apply make-up, a dash of cologne, and perhaps some simple earrings. Does wonders for your morale.

While children are napping, do something refreshing. Write, knit, or listen to pleasant music.

Your mind can accomplish things while your hands are busy

Do head work while dusting, sweeping, washing dishes, paring potatoes, etc. Plan family recreation, the garden, etc.

Have sink, work table, counter tops, etc. at a height that is comfortable, to eliminate strain . . . if dishpan is too low, set it on a box.

Prevent unnecessary fatigue

Use a dust mop and a long-handled dust pan. Use self-wringing mop (no stooping).

If you feel tired, lie down on the floor on your back, put your hands above your head, close your eyes, and relax for 3 to 5 min.

Exercise, sunshine, fresh air are part of health

Get outdoors every day. Take a walk, do some gardening, take the children for an outing, or pay your neighbor a short visit.

If you have just a moment, sit down, put your feet up on a chair, close your eyes and just relax your muscles. Let your arms, hands, and head fall limp.

Good posture prevents fatigue

When standing, keep erect posture . . . do not slump or bend over tasks (poor posture is more tiring). Remember sitting uses much less energy than standing.

Alternate sitting down tasks and standing up tasks. Don't be on your feet too long at one time.

Check up on yourself

If after following all these rules for proper rest, exercise, diet, you are still tired and depressed, have a medical check-up and follow doctor's orders.

Refresh your spirits

"Recreation" means "re-create" . . . for enthusiasm and courage. Garden, paint pictures, pursue any hobby, look through a magazine for home planning ideas, read a good book, or attend club meetings.

Harbor pleasant thoughts while working. It will make every task lighter and pleasanter.

Notice humorous and interesting incidents to relate at dinnertime, etc.

SERVE WITH FLAIR

(Betty Crocker Picture Cook Book, 1961)

If your main dish is a hearty one, serve a simple tossed salad, French bread or crusty rolls and light dessert. If less hearty, serve with a salad, vegetable, bread and a richer dessert.

It's fun to have several baking dishes in varying sizes, shapes and colors to suit your food—and your mood!

Garnishes are a welcome additional to main dishes. Keep a few sprigs of parsley in your refrigerator for a bright green touch. Sliced raw tomatoes, carrot curls and pickles, too, are colorful garnishes.

MEASURING

(Betty Crocker Picture Cook Book, 1950)

Cooking success is up to you! If you'll take pains to measure true, use standard cups and spoons all the way, and then level off—it'll always pay!

Use straight-edged knife for "leveling off."

Dry Measuring Cup has no rim . . . 1-cup line is even with the top. Use for any dry ingredients or shortening.

Liquid Measuring Cup . . . has rim above the 1-cup line. Use for measuring any liquid ingredients.

Graduated Measuring Cups . . . ¼, ⅓, ½, 1 cup. Use for part-cups of any dry ingredients or shortening.

Measuring Spoons . . . ¼, ½, 1 teaspoon and 1 tablespoon. Use for less than ½ cup of any ingredient.

EQUIPMENT

(Betty Crocker Picture Cook Book, 1950)

Just as every carpenter must have certain tools for building a house, every woman should have the right tools for the fine art of cooking. The size and needs of each household determine the kind and quantity that may be used for a number of purposes. Colorful utensils add a cherry note to the kitchen.

SATISFACTION

(Betty Crocker Picture Cook Book, 1950)

Good cooking and seasoning

Right combinations of food

Follow tested recipes carefully

Something soft and something crisp should always go together,

And something hot with something cold no matter what the weather;

Something bland needs the complement of something with tang and nip.

Follow these rules and all your meals will have taste, appeal and zip.

A MOTHER CAN GIVE HER FAMILY A PRICELESS GIFT

(Betty Crocker Picture Cook Book, 1950)

Why are some mothers tired all the time and some children fighting colds all winter? Probably because they don't eat the right things. Food that abundantly nourishes can make the difference between a family that just lives and one that has enough and more of health and vigor. You probably know this if you and your family are eating the right foods: all of you have the extra vitality to meet health hazards, the extra enthusiasm to welcome challenges and opportunities.

³⁴
MEAL-PLANNING

Check Your Daily Meals For:

SMART HOMEMAKERS SAY:

Planning, preparing, and serving meals is an *art* which develops through inspiration and thought. And meal-planning is really fun! It may look difficult to the beginner, but like driving a car, swimming, or anything we learn to do without thought or conscious effort, it is a skill which grows easier with the doing

It's important to plan a *variety* of foods for well balanced meals to keep your family well nourished. But above all, be sure those meals are appetizing, attractive, and delicious to eat. For mealtime should help build happy home life.

"My meals are more nutritious since I've been planning them ahead. I check in advance the basic foods and the daily needs of my family."

"Planning meals ahead helps me to save time and energy."

"I have made the cooking of meals a pleasure and a study rather than a job, and so I enjoy planning each day's menus."

"My meals are more interesting since I started planning ahead, because I avoid repetition and plan for variety in color, texture, and flavor."

I. APPROPRIATENESS
Cut your meal pattern to fit:

Your situation

The occasion

The family needs

"I always remember birthdays and holidays with a special dessert or color scheme."

"I plan the meals to be healthful for the children, first, and then interesting to adults, without cooking separate menus."

"We have a five-room bungalow with limited dining space and no help at all; this requires simplicity and informality."

"I plan my meals with the needs of my young son in mind. I never cook separately for him, but prepare simple foods appropriate for him and then dress them up for grown-up tastes and add to the menu to meet adult needs."

II. APPEARANCE

Prepare

Serve — each food attractively for greater appetite appeal

Present

"I think each meal out in detail, so there will be color appeal as well as good eating."

"When I was a child my father used to say, 'We should feast the eye as well as the appetite.' And it has become a tradition with me."

"In my kitchen windows I have many plants and I alternate them in decorating the table at mealtime."

CHAPTER ONE

Appetizers & Snacks

Olive-Cheese Balls

4 dozen cheese balls • Prep Time: 30 Minutes • Start to Finish: 1 Hour 50 Minutes

2 cups shredded sharp Cheddar cheese (8 oz)

1¼ cups all-purpose flour

½ cup butter, melted

48 small pimiento-stuffed olives, drained and patted dry

1 In large bowl, stir together cheese and flour. Stir in butter until mixture is thoroughly blended and smooth.

2 Mold 1 teaspoon dough around each olive; shape into ball. Place 2 inches apart on ungreased cookie sheet. Cover and refrigerate at least 1 hour but no longer than 24 hours.

3 Heat oven to 400°F. Bake 15 to 20 minutes or until light brown.

1 Cheese Ball: Calories 50; Total Fat 4g (Saturated Fat 2g, Trans Fat 0g); Cholesterol 10mg; Sodium 100mg; Total Carbohydrate 3g (Dietary Fiber 0g); Protein 1g **Exchanges:** 1 Fat **Carbohydrate Choices:** 0

Sausage Cheese Balls

8½ dozen cheese balls • Prep Time: 20 Minutes • Start to Finish: 45 Minutes

3 cups Original Bisquick™ mix

1 lb uncooked bulk pork sausage*

4 cups shredded Cheddar cheese (16 oz)

½ cup grated Parmesan cheese

½ cup milk

½ teaspoon dried rosemary, crushed

1½ teaspoons chopped fresh parsley or ½ teaspoon dried parsley flakes

Barbecue sauce or chili sauce, if desired

1 Heat oven to 350°F. Lightly grease bottom and sides of 15x10x1-inch pan. In large bowl, stir together all ingredients. Shape mixture into 1-inch balls. Place in pan.

2 Bake 20 to 25 minutes or until golden brown. Immediately remove cheese balls from pan. Serve warm with sauce for dipping.

*The recipe is correct as written; the mixture is made with uncooked sausage.

1 Cheese Ball: Calories 40; Total Fat 2.5g (Saturated Fat 1.5g, Trans Fat 0g); Cholesterol 5mg; Sodium 95mg; Total Carbohydrate 2g (Dietary Fiber 0g); Protein 2g **Exchanges:** ½ High-Fat Meat **Carbohydrate Choices:** 0

Deluxe Deviled Eggs

12 appetizers • Prep Time: 15 Minutes • Start to Finish: 30 Minutes

6   eggs

3   tablespoons mayonnaise, salad dressing or half-and-half

1   teaspoon prepared yellow, Dijon or spicy brown mustard*

1/8   teaspoon pepper

     Chopped fresh parsley

1. In 2-quart saucepan, place eggs in single layer. Cover with cold water at least 1 inch above eggs. Cover saucepan; heat to boiling.

2. Immediately remove from heat; let stand covered 15 minutes for large eggs (12 minutes for medium eggs and 18 minutes for extra-large eggs).

3. Drain. Immediately place eggs in cold water with ice cubes or run cold water over eggs until completely cooled.

4. To peel, gently tap egg on countertop until entire shell is finely crackled. Roll gently between hands to loosen shell. Starting at large end, peel egg under cold running water to help remove shell.

5. Cut lengthwise in half. Slip out yolks into small bowl; mash with fork. To prevent eggs from tipping on serving plate, cut a thin slice from bottom of each egg white half before filling. Or, to stand eggs upright, cut crosswise about two-thirds from top of narrow end of egg to remove yolk; cut thin slice from bottom of wide end of egg white to rest on serving platter.

6. Stir mayonnaise, mustard and pepper into yolks. Fill whites with egg yolk mixture, heaping lightly. Sprinkle with parsley. Cover and refrigerate up to 24 hours.

*Any flavored prepared mustard can be used, or 1/2 teaspoon ground mustard can be substituted for yellow mustard.

Bacon-Cheddar Deviled Eggs Mix 2 to 3 slices crisply cooked crumbled bacon and 2 tablespoons finely shredded Cheddar cheese into yolk mixture. Garnish with additional crumbled bacon or chopped fresh chives or parsley.

Blue Cheese Deviled Eggs Omit mustard. Mix ¼ cup crumbled blue cheese into yolk mixture. Garnish with coarsely ground black pepper and small celery leaves.

Chipotle Deviled Eggs Omit mustard. Mix 1½ to 2 teaspoons finely chopped chipotle chiles in adobo sauce (from 7-oz can), drained, and 1 thinly sliced green onion into yolk mixture. Garnish with whole or chopped cilantro.

Curried Deviled Eggs Omit mustard. Mix 2 tablespoons mango chutney (finely chop larger pieces of fruit if needed) and ¼ teaspoon curry powder into yolk mixture. Garnish with cashews or dry-roasted peanuts.

Fresh Herb Deviled Eggs Mix 1 teaspoon each chopped fresh chives, parsley and dill into yolk mixture. If desired, substitute basil or marjoram for the dill. Garnish with additional fresh herbs.

Ham and Veggie Deviled Eggs Mix 1 tablespoon each finely chopped red bell pepper, green bell pepper and cooked ham into yolk mixture. Garnish with additional chopped bell pepper.

Reuben Deviled Eggs Omit mustard. Substitute Thousand Island dressing for the mayonnaise. Stir in 2 tablespoons each finely chopped thinly sliced deli corned beef and finely chopped sauerkraut (squeezed in paper towel to drain). Garnish with shredded Swiss cheese and caraway seed.

Taco Deviled Eggs Omit mustard. Increase mayonnaise to ¼ cup. Mix 1 teaspoon dry taco seasoning mix into yolk mixture. Stir in 1 tablespoon well-drained chopped ripe olives, 2 tablespoons well-drained diced seeded tomato and 1 thinly sliced green onion. Garnish with a drizzle of taco sauce or small spoonful of salsa and diced avocado.

Wasabi Deviled Eggs Omit mustard. Mix 1 teaspoon wasabi paste and 1 teaspoon milk into yolk mixture. Garnish with thin slices pickled gingerroot, wasabi peas and black sesame seed.

Zesty Deviled Eggs Mix ½ cup finely shredded cheese, 2 tablespoons chopped fresh parsley and 1 to 2 teaspoons prepared horseradish into yolk mixture. Garnish with additional cheese or parsley.

BLAST FROM THE PAST:

Eggs—Are They Fresh?
(*Betty Crocker Picture Cook Book*, 1950)

Their shells should look dull . . .

Not shiny or bright;

But it makes no difference

If they're brown or they're white.

Savory Stuffed Mushrooms

36 appetizers • Prep Time: 20 Minutes • Start to Finish: 40 Minutes

36 medium mushrooms (1 lb)

2 tablespoons butter

1 small onion, chopped (¼ cup)

¼ cup chopped red bell pepper

1½ cups soft bread crumbs (about 2½ slices bread)

1½ teaspoons chopped fresh or ½ teaspoon dried thyme

½ teaspoon salt

¼ teaspoon ground turmeric

¼ teaspoon pepper

1 Heat oven to 350°F. Lightly spray 11x7-inch pan with cooking spray. Remove mushroom stems from mushroom caps. Finely chop enough stems to measure ⅓ cup. Reserve mushroom caps.

2 In 10-inch skillet, heat butter over medium-high heat. Add mushroom stems, onion and bell pepper to butter; cook about 5 minutes, stirring occasionally, until tender; remove from heat. Stir in all remaining ingredients. (To make ahead, cover and refrigerate filling up to 24 hours.)

3 With small spoon, fill each mushroom cap with bread crumb mixture. Place mushrooms, filled sides up, in pan. Bake uncovered 15 minutes.

4 Set oven to broil. Broil with tops 3 to 4 inches from heat about 2 minutes or until light brown. Serve warm.

1 Appetizer: Calories 30; Total Fat 1g (Saturated Fat 0g, Trans Fat 0g); Cholesterol 0mg; Sodium 70mg; Total Carbohydrate 4g (Dietary Fiber 0g); Protein 1g **Exchanges:** ½ Other Carbohydrate **Carbohydrate Choices:** 0

This cocktail sauce was in the first Betty Crocker cookbook in 1950, along with the shrimp in another chapter. Now they appear together and it just seems to be right!

Classic Shrimp Cocktail

6 servings • Prep Time: 30 Minutes • Start to Finish: 30 Minutes

SHRIMP

4 cups water

1½ lb uncooked large shrimp in shells, thawed if frozen, peeled (tail shells left on) and deveined

COCKTAIL SAUCE

1 cup ketchup

4 to 6 teaspoons prepared horseradish*

1 teaspoon Worcestershire sauce

2 or 3 drops red pepper sauce

GARNISH, IF DESIRED

Lemon slices

1 In 3-quart saucepan, heat water to boiling. Add shrimp. Cover and return to boiling; reduce heat. Simmer uncovered 3 to 5 minutes or until shrimp are pink; drain.

2 Meanwhile, in small bowl, mix sauce ingredients. Serve shrimp with sauce and lemon slices.

*Stir in 1 to 2 teaspoons additional horseradish if you like a spicier cocktail sauce.

1 Serving: Calories 100; Total Fat 0.5g (Saturated Fat 0g, Trans Fat 0g); Cholesterol 105mg; Sodium 770mg; Total Carbohydrate 11g (Dietary Fiber 0g); Protein 12g **Exchanges:** ½ Starch, 1½ Very Lean Meat **Carbohydrate Choices:** 1

MERRY KITSCHMAS PARTY

Mix it up—rather than throwing just another holiday party, why not make it a fun, vintage seasonal gathering? It will be a celebration your guests won't soon forget!

Start with a retro menu. Foods that evoke memories of childhood or holidays past are the building blocks for a successful event. How do you select a menu that your guests will love and leave you energetic and able to join the party? Choose recipes with a variety of different flavors, textures and colors. Include a few recipes that can be made ahead. Set the table ahead of time and get serving bowls and platters out and ready to fill.

Enlist the help of your guests when they arrive. Gone are the days where you are expected to do it all and make it look perfect. When you make people feel at home by allowing them to help, everyone relaxes a bit and you get to enjoy the party!

••• KITSCHMAS DINNER MENU •••
Olive-Cheese Balls (page 14) or
Sausage Cheese Balls (page 17)

Eggnog or punch (page 40, 43 or 44),
hot chocolate or hot toddies

Crown Roast of Pork (page 89) or
Baked Chicken Kiev (page 50)

Mashed potatoes

Mandarin Salad with Sugared Almonds (page 152)
or Waldorf Salad (page 147)

Refrigerator Potato Rolls (page 128)

Chocolate Cake Roll (page 187) or
Cherry Berries on a Cloud (page 221)

WHAT'S "KITSCHY"?
Anything vintage or retro can be kitschy! Old holiday flatware and china really bring the nostalgia to the food. Your family will love it if you use some dishes that were traditionally on the holiday table in years past. Antique dishes (non-holiday) can also be good choices.

OLD IS NEW
Make unexpected centerpieces from old lights, garlands and other decorations or tuck them in unexpected places around your entertaining areas. For a fun twist, mix and match newer decorations or lights with old ones. Twinkle lights are available in many sizes and colors to enhance your decorations. Using battery-operated lights means you don't have to hide any cords.

DRESS THE PART
Want to go the extra mile? Pick up a vintage dress and apron from a thrift store or online. What a great surprise for your guests (and it would quickly get them into the theme) to be greeted by a host or hostess dressed in vintage clothes—and don't forget the lipstick!

Cheese Ball

16 servings (2 tablespoons each) • Prep Time: 20 Minutes • Start to Finish: 10 Hours 50 Minutes

2   packages (8 oz each) cream cheese

¾   cup crumbled blue, Gorgonzola or feta cheese (4 oz)

1   cup shredded sharp Cheddar cheese (4 oz)

1   small onion, finely chopped (¼ cup)

1   tablespoon Worcestershire sauce

½   cup chopped fresh parsley

    Assorted crackers, if desired

1   Place cheeses in medium bowl; let stand at room temperature about 30 minutes or until softened.

2   Add onion and Worcestershire sauce to cheeses; beat with electric mixer on low speed until mixed. Beat on medium speed 1 to 2 minutes, scraping bowl frequently, until fluffy. Cover and refrigerate at least 8 hours or until firm enough to shape into a ball.

3   Shape cheese mixture into a large ball. Roll in parsley; place on serving plate. Cover and refrigerate about 2 hours or until firm. Serve with crackers.

1 Serving: Calories 160; Total Fat 14g (Saturated Fat 9g, Trans Fat 0g); Cholesterol 45mg; Sodium 240mg; Total Carbohydrate 2g (Dietary Fiber 0g); Protein 6g **Exchanges:** 1 High-Fat Meat, 1 Fat **Carbohydrate Choices:** 0

Smoked Salmon and Dill Canapés

12 servings (1 canapé) • Prep Time: 15 Minutes • Start to Finish: 2 Hours 15 Minutes

1 tablespoon lemon juice

½ cup cream cheese (half 8-oz container)

1 tablespoon chopped fresh dill weed

½ teaspoon garlic powder

12 slices cocktail rye or pumpernickel bread

3 oz salmon lox, cut into 12 pieces

1 tablespoon finely chopped red onion

Fresh dill weed sprigs, if desired

1 In small bowl, gradually stir lemon juice into cream cheese until smooth. Stir in chopped dill weed and garlic powder. Cover and refrigerate at least 2 hours but no longer than 24 hours.

2 Spread 2 teaspoons cheese mixture on each bread slice. Top each with salmon, onion and dill sprig.

1 Serving: Calories 60; Total Fat 4g (Saturated Fat 2g, Trans Fat 0g); Cholesterol 10mg; Sodium 125mg; Total Carbohydrate 4g (Dietary Fiber 0g); Protein 2g **Exchanges:** 1 Fat **Carbohydrate Choices:** 0

BETTY'S KITCHEN TIPS

If cocktail rye bread isn't available, try rye crackers instead.

Cold-smoked salmon, also called lox, comes in wafer-thin slices and doesn't flake into chunks the way hot-smoked salmon does.

BLAST FROM THE PAST:

(*Betty Crocker Picture Cook Book*, 1956)
Entertaining in Hollywood

Grace Kelly, winner of the Academy Award as the Best Moving Picture Actress of 1954, personally selected and sent us this menu as one of her favorites.

Caviar Blinis

Duck à l'Orange

French-Style Green Beans

Heart of Palm Salad Vinaigrette

Fruit

Cheese

Hot Crab Dip

2½ cups dip; 40 servings (1 tablespoon each) • Prep Time: 15 Minutes • Start to Finish: 35 Minutes

1 package (8 oz) cream cheese, softened

¼ cup grated Parmesan cheese

¼ cup mayonnaise or salad dressing

¼ cup dry white wine or nonalcoholic white wine

2 teaspoons sugar

1 teaspoon ground mustard

4 medium green onions, thinly sliced (¼ cup)

1 clove garlic, finely chopped

1 can (6 oz) crabmeat, drained, cartilage removed and flaked

⅓ cup sliced almonds, toasted*

Assorted crackers or fresh vegetables, if desired

1 Heat oven to 375°F. In medium bowl, stir together all ingredients except crabmeat, almonds and crackers until well blended. Stir in crabmeat.

2 Spread mixture in ungreased 9-inch pie plate or shallow 1-quart casserole. Sprinkle with almonds. Bake uncovered 15 to 20 minutes or until hot and bubbly. Serve warm with crackers.

*To toast almonds, spread in ungreased shallow pan. Bake uncovered at 350°F for 6 to 10 minutes, stirring occasionally, until light brown.

1 Serving: Calories 45; Total Fat 4g (Saturated Fat 1.5g, Trans Fat 0g); Cholesterol 10mg; Sodium 50mg; Total Carbohydrate 0g (Dietary Fiber 0g); Protein 2g
Exchanges: 1 Fat **Carbohydrate Choices:** 0

Creamy Shrimp Appetizers

32 servings (2 tablespoons dip and 1 red bell pepper piece each)
Prep Time: 25 Minutes • Start to Finish: 25 Minutes

1 package (8 oz) reduced-fat cream cheese (Neufchâtel), softened

3 to 4 tablespoons fat-free (skim) milk

1 teaspoon lemon-herb seasoning

1 can (about 4.25 oz) tiny shrimp, drained

1 tablespoon sliced green onion (1 medium)

1 tablespoon chopped green bell pepper

2 large red bell peppers, cut into 1½-inch pieces

32 leaves fresh Italian (flat-leaf) parsley

1 In small bowl, mix cream cheese, milk and lemon-herb seasoning until smooth. Add shrimp, green onion and green bell pepper; mix well.

2 Scoop mixture into red bell pepper pieces. Cover; refrigerate until serving time. Just before serving, top each with parsley leaf.

1 Serving: Calories 25; Total Fat 1.5g (Saturated Fat 1g, Trans Fat 0g); Cholesterol 10mg; Sodium 70mg; Total Carbohydrate 0g (Dietary Fiber 0g); Protein 1g **Exchanges:** ½ Fat **Carbohydrate Choices:** 0

BETTY'S KITCHEN TIP

Make the dip and refrigerate up to 8 hours ahead of time. Scoop onto pepper pieces just before serving.

Buy an extra can of shrimp and top each appetizer with 1 shrimp for added appeal.

Chicken Curry Spread

32 servings (2 tablespoons each) • Prep Time: 25 Minutes • Start to Finish: 25 Minutes

1 package (8 oz) reduced-fat cream cheese (Neufchâtel), softened

1 cup reduced-fat sour cream

1½ teaspoons curry powder

½ teaspoon salt

¼ teaspoon ground ginger

1 cup finely chopped cooked chicken breast

1 medium bell pepper, chopped (1 cup)

⅓ cup raisins

¼ cup sliced almonds, toasted*

Chopped fresh parsley, if desired

Apple and pear slices, if desired

1 In medium bowl, beat cream cheese, sour cream, curry powder, salt and ginger with spoon until smooth. Stir in chicken. Spread mixture on flat plate, about 9 to 10 inches in diameter.

2 Sprinkle bell pepper on cream cheese mixture. Sprinkle with raisins and almonds. Sprinkle parsley around edge. Serve with apple and pear slices.

*To toast almonds, spread in ungreased shallow pan. Bake uncovered at 350°F for 6 to 10 minutes, stirring occasionally, until light brown.

1 Serving: Calories 50; Total Fat 3g (Saturated Fat 1g, Trans Fat 1.5g); Cholesterol 12mg; Sodium 75mg; Total Carbohydrate 3g (Dietary Fiber 0g); Protein 3g **Exchanges:** ½ Lean Meat, ½ Fat **Carbohydrate Choices:** 0

BETTY'S KITCHEN TIP

This festive spread can be made up to 24 hours ahead of time. Add the almonds just before serving to prevent them from becoming soggy.

Havarti-Cheddar Fondue

20 servings (2 tablespoons fondue) • Prep Time: 30 Minutes • Start to Finish: 30 Minutes

1½ cups shredded Havarti cheese (6 oz)

1 cup shredded sharp Cheddar cheese (4 oz)

2 tablespoons all-purpose flour

½ cup chicken broth

⅓ cup milk

½ cup sliced drained sun-dried tomatoes in oil

4 medium green onions, sliced (¼ cup)

Dunkers (such as 1-inch bread cubes and cut-up fresh vegetables), if desired

1 In large resealable food-storage plastic bag, place cheeses and flour. Seal bag and shake until cheese is coated with flour. In fondue pot, heat broth and milk just to a simmer over warm/simmer setting (do not boil).

2 Add cheese mixture, about 1 cup at a time, stirring constantly with wire whisk until melted. Cook over warm/simmer setting, stirring constantly, until slightly thickened. Stir in tomatoes and green onions.

3 Keep fondue warm over warm/simmer setting. Serve with dunkers of your choice for dipping.

1 Serving: Calories 70; Total Fat 5g (Saturated Fat 3.5g, Trans Fat 0g); Cholesterol 15mg; Sodium 130mg; Total Carbohydrate 2g (Dietary Fiber 0g); Protein 3g **Exchanges:** ½ Medium-Fat Meat, ½ Fat **Carbohydrate Choices:** 0

BETTY'S KITCHEN TIP

Serve with broccoli florets, bell peppers, zucchini, sourdough bread cubes, breadsticks or pretzels for dipping into this cheesy fondue.

Oven Caramel Corn

15 servings (1 cup each) • Prep Time: 20 Minutes • Start to Finish: 1 Hour 50 Minutes

15 cups popped popcorn
½ cup butter
1 cup packed brown sugar
¼ cup light corn syrup
½ teaspoon salt
½ teaspoon baking soda

1 Heat oven to 200°F. Remove any unpopped kernels from popcorn. Place popcorn in very large roasting pan or very large bowl.

2 In 2-quart saucepan, melt butter over medium heat. Stir in brown sugar, corn syrup and salt. Heat to boiling, stirring occasionally. Continue cooking 5 minutes without stirring; remove from heat. Stir in baking soda until foamy.

3 Pour sugar mixture over popcorn; toss until evenly coated. If using bowl, transfer mixture to 2 ungreased 13x9-inch pans.

4 Bake uncovered 1 hour, stirring every 15 minutes. Spread on foil or cooking parchment paper (mixture will get crisp as it becomes completely cooled). Cool completely, about 30 minutes. Store tightly covered.

1 Serving: Calories 200; Total Fat 11g (Saturated Fat 4g, Trans Fat 0g); Cholesterol 15mg; Sodium 170mg; Total Carbohydrate 25g (Dietary Fiber 1g); Protein 1g **Exchanges:** ½ Starch, 1 Other Carbohydrate, 2 Fat **Carbohydrate Choices:** 1½

Nutty Caramel Corn Add 3 cups of pecans or walnuts with the popcorn.

Frosted Liverwurst Pâté

16 servings • Prep Time: 15 Minutes • Start to Finish: 8 Hours 15 Minutes

PÂTÉ

- 1 lb liverwurst or braunschweiger sausage
- 1 clove garlic, crushed
- ½ teaspoon dried basil
- ¼ cup finely chopped onion

TOPPING

- 1 package (8 oz) cream cheese, softened
- 1 clove garlic, crushed
- ¼ teaspoon hot pepper sauce
- 1 teaspoon mayonnaise or salad dressing

  Red or black caviar or anchovy paste

  Chopped fresh parsley

1 In medium bowl, mash liverwurst with fork. Add 1 clove garlic, basil and onion; mix well. Spoon onto serving plate, mounding to resemble igloo shape. Cover with plastic wrap; refrigerate while making topping.

2 In small bowl, mix cream cheese, 1 clove garlic, hot pepper sauce and mayonnaise until well blended. Spread mixture over liverwurst. Cover with plastic wrap; refrigerate at least 8 hours or until firm.

3 Just before serving, top with caviar or anchovy paste. Sprinkle with parsley.

1 Serving: Calories 150; Total Fat 13g (Saturated Fat 6g, Trans Fat 1g); Cholesterol 65mg; Sodium 310mg; Total Carbohydrate 2g (Dietary Fiber 0g); Protein 5g **Exchanges:** ½ High-Fat Meat, 2 Fat **Carbohydrate Choices:** 0

Orange Tea Mix

1½ cups mix • Prep Time: 10 Minutes • Start to Finish: 10 Minutes

6 tablespoons instant tea granules

2 envelopes (5 oz each) orange sugar-sweetened soft drink mix

1 In medium bowl, mix tea granules and drink mix. Store in tightly covered container for up to 1 month. For each serving, place 1 tablespoon mix in cup for hot tea or glass for cold tea. Fill cup with boiling water or glass with cold water; stir.

2 For 6 servings, place ⅓ cup mix in container (use heatproof container for hot tea). Add 4 cups boiling water for hot tea or 4 cups cold water for cold tea.

1 Tablespoon: Calories 50; Total Fat 0g (Saturated Fat 0g, Trans Fat 0g); Cholesterol 0mg; Sodium 5mg; Total Carbohydrate 12g (Dietary Fiber 0g); Protein 0g **Exchanges:** 1 Other Carbohydrate **Carbohydrate Choices:** 1

BLAST FROM THE PAST:

(*Betty Crocker Picture Cook Book*, 1956)
Tea

The glamour of centuries surrounds tea. Serving and drinking it has long been a ceremony in both China and Japan. It made its debut in England in 1666 as "tay." The London coffee houses that first served it soon became "tea" shops. "There are few hours of life more agreeable than the hour dedicated to afternoon tea," wrote an American novelist on his visit to England.

Frosty Citrus Punch

14 servings (about ¾ cup each) • Prep Time: 10 Minutes • Start to Finish: 10 Minutes

2 cans (12 oz each) frozen limeade or lemonade concentrate, thawed

6 cups cold water

1 bottle (2 liters) lemon-lime soda, chilled

1 pint (2 cups) lime or lemon sherbet

1 In large pitcher, mix limeade concentrate and water until blended.

2 Just before serving, stir in soda. Pour mixture into punch bowl. Spoon scoops of sherbet on top of punch.

1 Serving: Calories 190; Total Fat 1g (Saturated Fat 0g, Trans Fat 0g); Cholesterol 0mg; Sodium 30mg; Total Carbohydrate 46g (Dietary Fiber 0g); Protein 0g **Exchanges:** 3 Other Carbohydrate **Carbohydrate Choices:** 3

BETTY'S KITCHEN TIP

To make a simple lemon twist garnish, cut a long strip of peel with a vegetable peeler from around the lemon. Trim sides with a paring knife.

QUICK CRANBERRY PUNCH

12 servings (¾ cup each) • Prep Time: 10 Minutes • Start to Finish: 10 Minutes

1 can (6 oz) frozen pink lemonade concentrate, thawed

1 bottle (32 oz) cranberry juice cocktail, chilled

2 cans (12 oz each) ginger ale, chilled

1 In large pitcher, make lemonade as directed on can.

2 Stir in cranberry juice cocktail and enough ice to chill. Just before serving, stir in ginger ale.

1 Serving: Calories 90; Total Fat 0g (Saturated Fat 0g, Trans Fat 0g); Cholesterol 0mg; Sodium 10mg; Total Carbohydrate 23g (Dietary Fiber 0g); Protein 0g
Exchanges: 1½ Other Carbohydrate **Carbohydrate Choices:** 1½

BETTY'S KITCHEN TIP

Use additional cranberry juice to make ice cube swizzle sticks to keep glasses of your punch cold. Look for the swizzle stick ice molds in specialty kitchen stores, discount stores or online.

BLAST FROM THE PAST:

(*Betty Crocker Picture Cook Book*, 1950)
Clever Wife

The clever wife has a simple appetizing cocktail (cold in summer, hot in winter) ready for her weary husband when he comes home at night. Vegetable or fruit juices are at their best when two or three tart flavors are chilled and served ice cold in appropriate glasses.

The cool and refreshing rum-based daiquiri became popular in the United States after the world wars and Prohibition made whiskey harder to come by. Serving from a punch bowl was the rage in the 1950s and is finding a renewed interest today!

DAIQUIRI PUNCH

17 servings (½ cup each) • Prep Time: 15 Minutes • Start to Finish: 15 Minutes

2   cans (12 oz each) frozen limeade concentrate, thawed

2   cups lime-flavored sports drink, chilled

1   cup light rum

2   cans (12 oz each) lemon-lime carbonated beverage, chilled

1   In large pitcher, mix limeade concentrate, sports drink and rum. Refrigerate until serving time.

2   Just before serving, pour punch into punch bowl. Stir in carbonated beverage.

1 Serving: Calories 157; Total Fat 0g (Saturated Fat 0g, Trans Fat 0g); Cholesterol 0g; Sodium 15mg; Total Carbohydrate 31g (Dietary Fiber 0g); Protein 0g **Carbohydrate Choices:** 2

BETTY'S DO-AHEAD TIP

Mix the limeade concentrate, sports drink and rum, and refrigerate up to 24 hours. Your punch will be well chilled, and you won't rush at the last minute to prepare it.

BETTY'S KITCHEN TIP

Add holiday color and flavor to your punch with flavored ice cubes or small ice molds. Arrange small lime slices and maraschino cherry halves in ice cube trays or small molds. Pour lime-flavored sports drink over the fruit and freeze at least 2 hours.

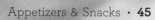

Manhattan Cocktails

2 servings • Prep Time: 5 Minutes • Start to Finish: 5 Minutes

2   maraschino cherries

¼   cup small ice cubes or shaved ice

⅓   cup bourbon or whiskey

⅓   cup sweet vermouth

2   dashes aromatic bitters

1 Chill 2 (3-oz) stemmed glasses in freezer.

2 Place cherry in each chilled glass. Place ice in martini shaker or pitcher. Add bourbon, vermouth and bitters; shake or stir to blend. Pour into glasses, straining out ice.

1 Serving: Calories 160; Total Fat 0g (Saturated Fat 0g, Trans Fat 0g); Cholesterol 0mg; Sodium 0mg; Total Carbohydrate 7g (Dietary Fiber 0g); Protein 0g
Carbohydrate Choices: ½

CHAPTER TWO

MAIN DISHES

> Although Chicken Kiev is traditionally fried, we have found that this baked version is just as delicious and is easy to make.

Baked Chicken Kiev

6 servings • Prep Time: 20 Minutes • Start to Finish: 1 Hour 25 Minutes

¼ cup butter, softened

1 tablespoon chopped fresh chives or parsley

1 clove garlic, finely chopped

6 boneless, skinless chicken breast halves (about 1¾ lb)

3 cups corn flake cereal, crushed (1½ cups)

2 tablespoons chopped fresh parsley

½ teaspoon paprika

¼ cup buttermilk or milk

1 In small bowl, mix butter, chives and garlic until well blended. Shape mixture into 3x2-inch rectangle. Cover and freeze about 30 minutes or until firm.

2 Heat oven to 425°F. Grease 9-inch square pan. Place each chicken breast half between sheets of plastic wrap or waxed paper. Lightly pound chicken, using flat side of meat mallet, until ¼ inch thick.

3 Cut butter mixture crosswise into 6 pieces. Place 1 piece butter on center of each chicken breast half. Fold long sides of chicken over butter. Fold ends up and secure each end with toothpick.

4 In shallow dish, mix corn flakes, parsley and paprika. Place buttermilk in another shallow dish. Dip chicken into buttermilk, then coat evenly with corn flake mixture. Place chicken, seam sides down, in pan.

5 Bake uncovered about 35 minutes or until chicken is no longer pink in center (when checking for doneness, be careful not to pierce all the way through chicken so butter mixture will not run out). Remove toothpicks.

1 Serving: Calories 330; Total Fat 13g (Saturated Fat 7g, Trans Fat 0g); Cholesterol 125mg; Sodium 270mg; Total Carbohydrate 13g (Dietary Fiber 0g); Protein 38g **Exchanges:** 1 Starch, 5 Very Lean Meat, 2 Fat **Carbohydrate Choices:** 1

BETTY'S KITCHEN TIP

Pair this delicious chicken dish with mashed potatoes, a green vegetable and dinner rolls for a nostalgic comfort meal.

Popular on menus for many years and named for the opera singer Luisa Tetrazzini, this combination of sauce, pasta and chicken is rich and delicious.

Chicken Tetrazzini

6 servings • Prep Time: 20 Minutes • Start to Finish: 50 Minutes

1 package (7 oz) spaghetti, broken into thirds

¼ cup butter

¼ cup all-purpose flour

½ teaspoon salt

¼ teaspoon pepper

1 cup chicken broth

1 cup whipping cream

2 tablespoons dry sherry or water

2 cups cubed cooked chicken or turkey

1 jar (4.5 oz) sliced mushrooms, drained

½ cup grated Parmesan cheese

Chopped fresh parsley, if desired

1 Heat oven to 350°F. Cook and drain spaghetti as directed on package, using minimum cook time.

2 Meanwhile, in 2-quart saucepan, melt butter over low heat. Stir in flour, salt and pepper. Cook and stir until mixture is smooth and bubbly; remove from heat. Stir in broth and whipping cream. Heat to boiling, stirring constantly. Boil and stir 1 minute.

3 Stir spaghetti, sherry, chicken and mushrooms into sauce. Spoon into ungreased 2-quart casserole. Sprinkle with cheese. Bake uncovered about 30 minutes or until bubbly in center. Sprinkle with parsley.

1 Serving: Calories 470; Total Fat 27g (Saturated Fat 14g, Trans Fat 1g); Cholesterol 110mg; Sodium 810mg; Total Carbohydrate 33g (Dietary Fiber 2g); Protein 23g **Exchanges:** 2 Starch, 2½ Medium-Fat Meat, 2½ Fat **Carbohydrate Choices:** 2

Chicken Pot Pie

6 servings • Prep Time: 40 Minutes • Start to Finish: 1 Hour 15 Minutes

1 box refrigerated pie crusts, softened as directed on box

⅓ cup butter

⅓ cup all-purpose flour

⅓ cup chopped onion

½ teaspoon salt

¼ teaspoon pepper

1¾ cups chicken broth

⅔ cup milk

2½ to 3 cups cut-up cooked chicken

1 package (10 oz) frozen peas and carrots, thawed, drained

1 Heat oven to 425°F. Remove 1 pie crust from pouch; roll into 13-inch square. Ease into ungreased 8-inch square (2-quart) glass baking dish.

2 In 2-quart saucepan, melt butter over medium heat. Stir in flour, onion, salt and pepper. Cook and stir until mixture is bubbly; remove from heat. Stir in broth and milk. Heat to boiling, stirring constantly. Boil and stir 1 minute. Stir in chicken and frozen vegetables. Pour mixture into crust-lined dish.

3 Roll remaining pie crust into 11-inch square. With 1-inch cookie cutter, cut shapes in crust. Place crust over chicken mixture; seal and flute edges. Arrange cutouts on crust.

4 Bake 35 to 40 minutes or until filling is bubbly and crust is golden brown.

1 Serving: Calories 670; Total Fat 43g (Saturated Fat 14g, Trans Fat 5g); Cholesterol 80mg; Sodium 1050mg; Total Carbohydrate 44g (Dietary Fiber 3g); Protein 25g **Exchanges:** 3 Starch, 2½ Lean Meat, 6½ Fat **Carbohydrate Choices:** 3

Skillet-Fried Chicken

6 servings • Prep Time: 10 Minutes • Start to Finish: 40 Minutes

½ cup all-purpose flour

1 tablespoon paprika

1½ teaspoons salt

½ teaspoon pepper

1 whole chicken, cut up
  (3 to 3½ lb)

  Vegetable oil

1 In shallow dish, mix flour, paprika, salt and pepper. Coat chicken with flour mixture.

2 In 12-inch nonstick skillet, heat oil (¼ inch) over medium-high heat. Add chicken, skin side down; cook about 10 minutes or until light brown on all sides.

3 Reduce heat to low. Turn chicken skin side up. Simmer uncovered about 20 minutes, without turning, until juice of chicken is clear when thickest piece is cut to bone (at least 165°F on meat thermometer).

1 Serving: Calories 330; Total Fat 20g (Saturated Fat 4.5g, Trans Fat 0g); Cholesterol 85mg; Sodium 670mg; Total Carbohydrate 9g (Dietary Fiber 0g); Protein 28g **Exchanges:** ½ Starch, 4 Medium-Fat Meat **Carbohydrate Choices:** ½

RETRO TIKI PARTY

This fun themed party will give guests a chance to dust off their favorite sundress or Hawaiian shirt and enjoy a bit of "warm" weather, even when it's cold outside!

SET THE STAGE

- **Select the foods you will have at the party.** Having just a few dishes can pull off the theme. Build your menu around a few "stars": Caribbean Chicken Kabobs (page 60), Mango Pork Fried Rice (page 170) and Triple-Threat Coconut Cream Pie (page 208) are great choices. Add an appetizer and a green salad, and dinner is set! (Or ask guests to bring the appetizers and salad to make it easier on you.)

- **Serving foods in food containers was big.** Use hollowed-out pineapple halves, coconuts or bell peppers as serving bowls. You could even make "palm trees" from a carrot and bell pepper as the beachy decoration for a simple veggie or cheese and crackers tray.

- **Rum punch, anyone?** Choose a tropical drink or two to serve at the party. If you have the ingredients chilled, simply pour them into punch bowls or beverage servers, so guests can help themselves. If you don't have large beverage servers, borrow them from people who have had graduation parties—chances are, they have purchased at least one!

- **Offer paper umbrellas,** small picks with a chunk of pineapple and a maraschino cherry or swizzle sticks to garnish the glasses, just like you'd get on a tropical vacation. Want guests to mix and mingle? Set up the bar in an area that's different from where the food is.

- **Nothing sets the mood quicker** than scents and sounds. Have a coconut or hibiscus candle burning in your entryway, so guests will be greeted by the subtle scent when they arrive. Have island music playing in the background. Scan free Internet or cable/satellite radio channels for appropriate music.

- **Offer inexpensive leis** near the front door, for guests to put on when they arrive. Look for them at dollar stores, party stores or online.

- **Decorate with brightly colored tablecloths,** runners or napkins. Mats that are woven or have bamboo or wood accents also go with the theme. Brightly colored flowers and fresh tropical fruit like pineapples and coconuts make fun decorations.

Caribbean Chicken Kabobs

8 servings • Prep Time: 30 Minutes • Start to Finish: 30 Minutes

1¾ lb boneless skinless chicken breasts, cut into 1½-inch pieces

¼ cup vegetable oil

3 tablespoons Caribbean jerk seasoning (dry)

1 small pineapple, rind and core removed, cut into 1-inch cubes

1 medium red bell pepper, cut into 1-inch pieces

1 small red onion, cut into 1-inch pieces

1 Heat gas or charcoal grill. Brush chicken with 2 tablespoons of the oil. Place chicken and jerk seasoning in resealable food-storage plastic bag. Seal bag; shake to coat chicken with seasoning.

2 On each of 8 (12-inch) metal skewers, alternately thread chicken, pineapple, bell pepper and onion, leaving ¼ inch space between each piece. Brush kabobs with remaining 2 tablespoons oil.

3 Place kabobs on grill over medium heat. Cover grill; cook 10 to 15 minutes, turning once, until chicken is no longer pink in center.

1 Serving: Calories 210; Total Fat 10g (Saturated Fat 2g, Trans Fat 0g); Cholesterol 60mg; Sodium 210mg; Total Carbohydrate 8g (Dietary Fiber 1g); Protein 22g **Exchanges:** ½ Other Carbohydrate, 3 Very Lean Meat, 1½ Fat **Carbohydrate Choices:** ½

Party Waffles Royale

6 servings • Prep Time: 20 Minutes • Start to Finish: 35 Minutes

CREAMED CHICKEN

- ¼ cup butter
- ¼ cup Original Bisquick mix
- ½ teaspoon salt
- ¼ teaspoon pepper
- ¼ teaspoon poultry seasoning
- 2 cups milk
- 2 cups cut-up cooked chicken

WAFFLES

- 2 cups Original Bisquick mix
- 1⅓ cups plus 2 tablespoons milk
- 1 tablespoon vegetable oil
- 1 egg

SERVE WITH

- ¾ cup whole-berry cranberry sauce, warmed

  Sprigs of fresh thyme and additional pepper, if desired

1 In 3-quart saucepan, melt butter over low heat. Blend in Bisquick mix and seasonings. Cook over low heat, stirring, until mixture is bubbly. Stir in 1⅓ cups of the milk. Heat to boiling over medium heat, stirring constantly. Boil 1 minute. (If sauce seems too thick, add remaining milk, 1 tablespoon at a time, until desired consistency is reached.) Stir in chicken; heat through. Keep warm while making waffles.

2 Heat waffle iron; grease with vegetable oil if necessary. In medium bowl, beat all waffle ingredients together until blended. Pour batter into center of hot waffle iron. Close lid of waffle iron. Bake until steaming stops. Carefully remove waffle with fork.

3 To serve, arrange 2 waffles on plate. Pour about ½ cup creamed chicken on top. Serve with warm cranberry sauce. Garnish with thyme and pepper.

1 Serving: Calories 490; Total Fat 24g (Saturated Fat 12g, Trans Fat 0.5g); Cholesterol 105mg; Sodium 920mg; Total Carbohydrate 47g (Dietary Fiber 0g); Protein 22g **Exchanges:** 1 Starch, 1½ Other Carbohydrate, ½ Low-Fat Milk, 2 Lean Meat, 3 Fat **Carbohydrate Choices:** 3

Turkey Divan

6 servings • Prep Time: 40 Minutes • Start to Finish: 40 Minutes

1½ lb fresh broccoli*

¼ cup butter

¼ cup all-purpose flour

⅛ teaspoon ground nutmeg

1½ cups chicken broth

1 cup grated Parmesan cheese

½ cup whipping cream

2 tablespoons dry white wine or chicken broth

6 large slices cooked turkey or chicken breast, ¼ inch thick (¾ lb)

1 Cut broccoli lengthwise into ½-inch-wide spears. In 2-quart saucepan, heat 1 inch water (salted if desired) to boiling. Add broccoli. Heat to boiling. Boil uncovered 5 minutes; drain, remove from pot and keep warm.

2 In same saucepan, melt butter over medium heat. Stir in flour and nutmeg. Cook, stirring constantly, until smooth and bubbly; remove from heat. Stir in broth. Heat to boiling, stirring constantly. Boil and stir 1 minute; remove from heat. Stir in ½ cup of the cheese, whipping cream and wine.

3 Place hot broccoli in ungreased 11x7-inch (2-quart) glass baking dish. Top with turkey. Pour cheese sauce over turkey. Sprinkle with remaining ½ cup cheese.

4 Set oven to broil. Broil with top 3 to 5 inches from heat about 3 minutes or until cheese is bubbly and light brown.

*Two packages (9 oz each) frozen broccoli spears, cooked and drained, can be substituted for the fresh broccoli.

1 Serving: Calories 350; Total Fat 22g (Saturated Fat 12g, Trans Fat 1g); Cholesterol 105mg; Sodium 690mg; Total Carbohydrate 9g (Dietary Fiber 3g); Protein 29g **Exchanges:** 2 Vegetable, 3 Lean Meat, 2 Fat **Carbohydrate Choices:** ½

TEXAS HASH

4 servings • Prep Time: 25 Minutes • Start to Finish: 45 Minutes

2 tablespoons vegetable oil

1 cup chopped onion

1 cup chopped green bell pepper

1 lb lean (at least 80%) ground beef

2 cups water

1 cup uncooked long-grain white rice

1½ teaspoons chili powder

½ teaspoon salt

⅛ teaspoon pepper

1 can (14.5 oz) diced tomatoes, undrained

1 In 10-inch nonstick skillet, heat oil over medium-high heat. Add onion and bell pepper; cook about 5 minutes or until very tender, stirring occasionally. Add ground beef; cook 8 to 10 minutes or until beef is thoroughly cooked, stirring occasionally. Drain fat from skillet if necessary.

2 Stir in water, rice, chili powder, salt, pepper and tomatoes. Reduce heat; cover and simmer about 20 minutes or until rice is tender, stirring occasionally.

1 Serving: Calories 480; Total Fat 20g (Saturated Fat 6g, Trans Fat 0.5g); Cholesterol 70mg; Sodium 530mg; Total Carbohydrate 50g (Dietary Fiber 3g); Protein 25g **Exchanges:** 3 Starch, 1 Vegetable, 2 Lean Meat, 2½ Fat **Carbohydrate Choices:** 3

BLAST FROM THE PAST:

(*Betty Crocker Picture Cook Book*, 1950)
Original Tip for Rice Ring

All you have to do to make a Rice Ring: lightly press 2 cups fluffy boiled rice (⅔ cup uncooked) into well-greased 10-inch ring mold. Keep hot until time to serve. Unmold on hot platter and fill center with creamed seafood or chicken and mushrooms. Serve hot. Serves 8 to 10.

STUFFED PEPPERS

4 servings • Prep Time: 15 Minutes • Start to Finish: 55 Minutes

4   large bell peppers
    (any color)

1   lb lean (at least 80%)
    ground beef

2   tablespoons chopped onion

1   cup cooked rice

1   teaspoon salt

1   clove garlic, finely chopped

1   can (15 oz) tomato sauce

¾   cup shredded mozzarella
    cheese (3 oz)

1 Heat oven to 350°F. Cut thin slice from stem end of each bell pepper to remove top of pepper. Remove seeds and membranes; rinse peppers. If necessary, cut thin slice from bottom of each pepper so they stand up straight. In 4-quart Dutch oven or large saucepan, add enough water to cover peppers. Heat to boiling; add peppers. Cook about 2 minutes; drain.

2 In 10-inch skillet, cook ground beef and onion over medium heat 8 to 10 minutes, stirring occasionally, until beef is brown; drain. Stir in rice, salt, garlic and 1 cup of the tomato sauce; cook and stir over medium heat until mixture begins to boil. Remove from heat.

3 Stuff peppers with beef mixture. Stand peppers upright in ungreased 8-inch square (2-quart) glass baking dish. Pour remaining tomato sauce over peppers.

4 Cover tightly with foil. Bake 10 minutes. Uncover and bake about 15 minutes longer or until peppers are tender. Sprinkle with cheese.

1 Serving: Calories 390; Total Fat 17g (Saturated Fat 7g, Trans Fat 1g); Cholesterol 80mg; Sodium 1470mg; Total Carbohydrate 29g (Dietary Fiber 4g); Protein 29g **Exchanges:** ½ Starch, ½ Other Carbohydrate, 3 Vegetable, 2½ Lean Meat, ½ Medium-Fat Meat, 1½ Fat **Carbohydrate Choices:** 2

Originally appearing in the first edition of the Betty Crocker cookbook in 1950, this recipe continued to be printed in several more editions over the years.

SWEDISH MEATBALLS

6 servings (about 4 meatballs and ⅓ cup sauce) • Prep Time: 1 Hour 10 Minutes
Start to Finish: 1 Hour 10 Minutes

MEATBALLS

- 1 lb lean (at least 80%) ground beef
- ½ lb lean ground pork
- 1 small onion, finely chopped (½ cup)
- ¾ cup plain panko bread crumbs
- 2 tablespoons finely chopped fresh parsley
- ½ teaspoon salt
- ⅛ teaspoon pepper
- 1 teaspoon Worcestershire sauce
- 1 egg
- ½ cup milk

GRAVY

- ¼ cup butter
- ¼ cup all-purpose flour
- 1 teaspoon paprika
- ¼ teaspoon salt
- ⅛ teaspoon pepper
- 2 cups water
- ¾ cup sour cream

1 In large bowl, mix all meatball ingredients until well blended. Shape into 1½-inch meatballs. Place meatballs in large skillet; cook over medium heat 8 to 10 minutes or until browned. Remove meatballs from skillet; cover to keep warm.

2 In same skillet, melt butter over medium heat. With wire whisk, stir in flour, paprika, salt and pepper; cook, stirring, until bubbly. Slowly add water, stirring constantly until mixture boils and thickens. Add meatballs to gravy. Cook over medium-low heat 8 to 10 minutes or until meatballs are thoroughly cooked. Stir in sour cream until blended and hot.

1 Serving: Calories 430; Total Fat 29g (Saturated Fat 14g, Trans Fat 1g); Cholesterol 140mg; Sodium 490mg; Total Carbohydrate 17g (Dietary Fiber 0g); Protein 25g **Exchanges:** 1 Other Carbohydrate, 3½ Lean Meat, 3½ Fat **Carbohydrate Choices:** 1

CREAMY GROUND BEEF-NOODLE CASSEROLE

8 servings • Prep Time: 30 Minutes • Start to Finish: 1 Hour

8   oz uncooked farfalle pasta (about 2½ cups)

1   lb ground beef

1   can (15 oz) tomato sauce

½   teaspoon garlic salt

¼   teaspoon black pepper

1   cup sour cream

1   cup cottage cheese

½   cup shredded Parmesan cheese

¾   cup sliced green onions

1½   cups shredded Cheddar cheese (12 oz)

1   Heat oven to 350°F. Spray 13x9-inch baking dish or 2½- to 3-quart casserole with cooking spray. Cook pasta according to package directions until al dente, about 11 minutes; drain, and set aside.

2   Meanwhile, in 10-inch nonstick skillet, cook beef over medium-high heat 5 to 7 minutes, stirring frequently, until no longer pink; drain. Stir in tomato sauce, garlic salt and pepper; cover and simmer 2 to 3 minutes or until slightly thickened.

3   In large bowl, mix sour cream, cottage cheese, Parmesan cheese and ½ cup of the green onions; stir in cooked pasta.

4   Spoon half of the pasta mixture into baking dish. Top with half of the beef mixture and ¾ cup of the Cheddar cheese. Repeat with pasta mixture, beef mixture and remaining ¾ cup Cheddar cheese. Bake uncovered 25 to 30 minutes or until mixture is thoroughly heated and cheese is melted. Top with remaining ¼ cup green onions and serve.

1 Serving: Calories 430; Total Fat 22g (Saturated Fat 11g, Trans Fat 1g); Cholesterol 80mg; Sodium 810mg; Total Carbohydrate 30g (Dietary Fiber 2g); Protein 26g **Exchanges:** 1 Starch, 1 Other Carbohydrate, ½ Vegetable, 1½ Lean Meat, ½ Medium-Fat Meat, 1 High-Fat Meat, 1½ Fat **Carbohydrate Choices:** 2

BETTY'S KITCHEN TIP

Wide egg noodles or Mafalda pasta would also work in this recipe. Stir ½ teaspoon crushed red pepper into beef mixture for a spicy kick.

Beef Stroganoff

6 servings • Prep Time: 25 Minutes • Start to Finish: 50 Minutes

1½ lb beef tenderloin or boneless top sirloin steak

2 tablespoons butter

1½ cups beef broth

2 tablespoons ketchup

1 teaspoon salt

1 clove garlic, finely chopped

1 package (8 oz) sliced fresh mushrooms (about 3 cups)

1 medium onion, chopped (½ cup)

¼ cup all-purpose flour

1 cup sour cream or plain yogurt

Hot cooked noodles or rice, if desired

Parsley, if desired

1 Cut beef across grain into 1½x½-inch strips (beef is easier to cut if partially frozen). In 12-inch skillet, melt butter over medium-high heat. Cook beef in butter, stirring occasionally, until brown.

2 Reserve ⅓ cup of the broth. Stir remaining broth, ketchup, salt and garlic into beef. Heat to boiling; reduce heat. Cover and simmer about 10 minutes or until beef is tender.

3 Stir in mushrooms and onion. Heat to boiling; reduce heat. Cover and simmer about 5 minutes longer or until onion is tender.

4 In tightly covered container, shake reserved ⅓ cup broth and flour until mixed; gradually stir into beef mixture. Heat to boiling, stirring constantly. Boil and stir 1 minute; reduce heat to low. Stir in sour cream; heat until hot. Serve over noodles. Sprinkle with parsley.

1 Serving: Calories 330; Total Fat 20g (Saturated Fat 10g, Trans Fat 1g); Cholesterol 100mg; Sodium 810mg; Total Carbohydrate 10g (Dietary Fiber 1g); Protein 28g **Exchanges:** 2 Vegetable, 3½ Lean Meat, 1 Fat **Carbohydrate Choices:** ½

Many recipes from the first Big Reds showcased ways to make economical cuts of meat seem like better cuts. Here, "steak" was made by simmering a tougher cut with savory ingredients to make it as tender as a good steak.

Swiss Steak

6 servings • Prep Time: 15 Minutes • Start to Finish: 1 Hour 55 Minutes

1 boneless beef round, tip or chuck steak, about ¾ inch thick (1½ lb)

3 tablespoons all-purpose flour

1 teaspoon ground mustard

½ teaspoon salt

2 tablespoons vegetable oil

1 can (14.5 oz) diced tomatoes, undrained

2 cloves garlic, finely chopped

1 cup water

1 large onion, cut in half, sliced

1 large green bell pepper, sliced

1 Cut beef into 6 serving pieces. In small bowl, mix flour, mustard and salt. Sprinkle half of the flour mixture over one side of beef; pound in with meat mallet. Turn beef; pound in remaining flour mixture.

2 In 10-inch skillet, heat oil over medium heat. Cook beef in oil about 15 minutes, turning once, until brown.

3 Stir in tomatoes and garlic. Heat to boiling; reduce heat. Cover and simmer about 1 hour 15 minutes, occasionally spooning sauce over beef, until beef is tender.

4 Add water, onion and bell pepper. Heat to boiling; reduce heat. Cover and simmer 5 to 8 minutes longer or until vegetables are tender.

1 Serving: Calories 210; Total Fat 8g (Saturated Fat 2g, Trans Fat 0g); Cholesterol 60mg; Sodium 340mg; Total Carbohydrate 10g (Dietary Fiber 2g); Protein 24g **Exchanges:** 2 Vegetable, 3 Lean Meat **Carbohydrate Choices:** ½

MEAT LOAF

6 servings • Prep Time: 20 Minutes • Start to Finish: 1 Hour 40 Minutes

1 egg, beaten

1 cup milk

1 tablespoon Worcestershire sauce

1½ lb lean (at least 80%) ground beef

3 slices bread, finely chopped (1½ cups lightly packed)

1 small onion, chopped (¼ cup)

½ teaspoon salt

½ teaspoon ground mustard

¼ teaspoon pepper

½ cup ketchup, chili sauce or barbecue sauce

1 Heat oven to 350°F. In large bowl, mix all ingredients except ketchup. Spread mixture in ungreased 9x5-inch loaf pan, or shape into 9x5-inch loaf in ungreased 13x9-inch pan. Spread ketchup over top.

2 Insert ovenproof meat thermometer so tip is in center of loaf. Bake uncovered 1 hour to 1 hour 15 minutes or until thermometer reads at least 160°F.

3 Drain meat loaf. Let stand 5 minutes. Remove from pan.

1 Serving: Calories 290; Total Fat 15g (Saturated Fat 6g, Trans Fat 1g); Cholesterol 110mg; Sodium 610mg; Total Carbohydrate 15g (Dietary Fiber 0g); Protein 24g **Exchanges:** 1 Starch, 3 Medium-Fat Meat, ½ Fat **Carbohydrate Choices:** 1

BLAST FROM THE PAST:

(*Betty Crocker Picture Cook Book*, 1950)
Make Ground Meat Go Further

To make ground meat go further, mix it with Wheaties™, bread or cracker crumbs, cooked rice or oatmeal and milk to moisten.

Beef Fajitas

6 servings • Prep Time: 1 Hour • Start to Finish: 9 Hours

MARINADE

- ¼ cup vegetable oil
- ¼ cup red wine vinegar
- 1 teaspoon sugar
- 1 teaspoon dried oregano
- 1 teaspoon chili powder
- ½ teaspoon garlic powder
- ½ teaspoon salt
- ¼ teaspoon pepper

FAJITAS

- 1 boneless beef top sirloin steak, 1½ inches thick (1½ lb), trimmed of excess fat
- 2 large onions, sliced
- 2 medium green or red bell peppers, cut into ¼-inch strips
- 2 tablespoons vegetable oil
- 12 flour tortillas (9 or 10 inches)
- 1 jar (8 oz) picante sauce (1 cup)
- 1 cup shredded Cheddar or Monterey Jack cheese (4 oz)
- 1½ cups guacamole
- ¾ cup sour cream

1. In shallow glass or plastic dish, mix all marinade ingredients. Pierce beef with fork in several places. Add beef to marinade in dish; turn to coat. Cover and refrigerate at least 8 hours but no longer than 24 hours, turning occasionally.

2. Heat gas or charcoal grill. In large bowl, toss onions and bell peppers with oil; place in grill basket (grill "wok"). Set aside.

3. Remove beef from marinade; reserve marinade. Place beef on grill over medium heat. Cover grill; cook 22 to 26 minutes for medium-rare (145°F) to medium doneness (160°F), turning once and brushing occasionally with reserved marinade. Add vegetables to grill for last 6 to 8 minutes of cooking, shaking basket or stirring vegetables once or twice, until crisp-tender.

4. Meanwhile, heat oven to 325°F. Wrap tortillas in foil. Heat in oven about 15 minutes or until warm. Remove tortillas from oven; keep wrapped.

5. Discard any remaining marinade. Cut beef across grain into very thin slices. For each fajita, place a few slices of beef, some of the onion mixture, 1 heaping tablespoonful each picante sauce and cheese, 2 tablespoons guacamole and 1 tablespoon sour cream on center of tortilla. Fold 1 end of tortilla up about 1 inch over filling; fold right and left sides over folded end, overlapping. Fold remaining end down.

1 Serving: Calories 790; Total Fat 34g (Saturated Fat 12g, Trans Fat 2g); Cholesterol 95mg; Sodium 1590mg; Total Carbohydrate 78g (Dietary Fiber 7g); Protein 41g **Exchanges:** 4 Starch, ½ Other Carbohydrate, 1½ Vegetable, 3½ Lean Meat, 4½ Fat **Carbohydrate Choices:** 5

Spreading a layer of horseradish all over the outside of the meat is the secret to making this pot roast. Contrary to what you might think, the horseradish doesn't add a hot or spicy flavor. Instead, it mellows during cooking, leaving behind a delicious flavor.

Pot Roast

. . . .

8 servings • Prep Time: 30 Minutes • Start to Finish: 4 Hours

. . . .

1 boneless beef chuck, arm, shoulder or blade pot roast (4 lb)*

1 teaspoon salt

1 teaspoon pepper

1 jar (8 oz) prepared horseradish

1 cup water

8 small potatoes, cut in half

8 medium carrots or parsnips, peeled, cut into quarters

8 small whole onions, peeled

½ cup cold water

¼ cup all-purpose flour

Parsley, if desired

1 In 4-quart Dutch oven or large saucepan, cook beef over medium heat until brown on all sides; reduce heat to low.

2 Sprinkle beef with salt and pepper. Spread horseradish over all sides of beef. Add 1 cup water to Dutch oven. Heat to boiling; reduce heat. Cover and simmer 2 hours 30 minutes.

3 Add potatoes, carrots and onions to Dutch oven. Cover and simmer about 1 hour longer or until beef and vegetables are tender.

4 Remove beef and vegetables to warm platter; cover to keep warm. Skim excess fat from broth in Dutch oven. Add enough water to broth to measure 2 cups. In tightly covered container, shake ½ cup cold water and the flour; gradually stir into broth. Heat to boiling, stirring constantly. Boil and stir 1 minute. Serve gravy with beef and vegetables; sprinkle with parsley.

*A 3-lb beef bottom round, rolled rump, tip or chuck eye roast can be used; reduce salt to ¾ teaspoon.

1 Serving: Calories 590; Total Fat 24g (Saturated Fat 9g, Trans Fat 1g); Cholesterol 145mg; Sodium 560mg; Total Carbohydrate 47g (Dietary Fiber 7g); Protein 46g **Exchanges:** 1 Starch, 1½ Other Carbohydrate, 1½ Vegetable, 5½ Lean Meat, 1½ Fat **Carbohydrate Choices:** 3

Confetti Pot Roast Omit horseradish and potatoes. Sprinkle beef with ½ teaspoon Italian seasoning. Add ½ pound fresh green beans and 1 cup frozen corn with the carrots in Step 3. Continue as directed. Serve with mashed potatoes.

Cream Gravy Pot Roast Substitute 1 can (10½ oz) condensed beef broth for the 1 cup water. For the gravy, add enough half-and-half or milk, instead of water, to the cooking liquid to measure 2 cups. Substitute ½ cup half-and-half or milk for the ½ cup cold water.

Garlic-Herb Pot Roast Reduce pepper to ½ teaspoon. Omit horseradish. After browning the beef in Step 1, sprinkle with 1 tablespoon chopped fresh or 1 teaspoon dried marjoram, 1 tablespoon chopped fresh or 1 teaspoon dried thyme, 2 teaspoons chopped fresh or ½ teaspoon dried oregano and 4 cloves garlic, finely chopped. Substitute 1 can (10½ oz) condensed beef broth for the 1 cup water.

Beef Stew

8 servings • Prep Time: 15 Minutes • Start to Finish: 3 Hours 45 Minutes

1   lb beef stew meat, cut into ½-inch pieces

1   medium onion, cut into 8 wedges

1   bag (8 oz) ready-to-eat baby-cut carrots (about 30)

1   can (14.5 oz) diced tomatoes, undrained

1   can (10.5 oz) condensed beef broth

1   can (8 oz) tomato sauce

⅓   cup all-purpose flour

1   tablespoon Worcestershire sauce

1   teaspoon salt

1   teaspoon sugar

1   teaspoon dried marjoram

¼   teaspoon pepper

12   small red potatoes (1½ lb), cut into quarters

2   cups sliced fresh mushrooms (about 5 oz) or 1 package (about 3.5 oz) fresh shiitake mushrooms, sliced

1   Heat oven to 325°F. In 4-quart ovenproof Dutch oven or roaster, mix all ingredients except potatoes and mushrooms. Cover and bake 2 hours, stirring once.

2   Stir in potatoes and mushrooms. Cover and bake 1 hour to 1 hour 30 minutes longer or until beef and vegetables are tender.

1 Serving: Calories 310; Total Fat 7g (Saturated Fat 2.5g, Trans Fat 0g); Cholesterol 35mg; Sodium 820mg; Total Carbohydrate 43g (Dietary Fiber 6g); Protein 18g **Exchanges:** 2 Starch, 2 Vegetable, 1 Medium-Fat Meat, ½ Fat **Carbohydrate Choices:** 3

Slow Cooker Sauerbraten Beef

6 servings (2 cups each) • Prep Time: 20 Minutes • Start to Finish: 7 Hours 35 Minutes

2 lb beef stew meat
   (1-inch pieces)

1 cup chopped onions
   (2 medium)

1 cup beef broth

1 cup red wine vinegar or
   cider vinegar

2 dried bay leaves

6 cups uncooked medium egg
   noodles (12 oz)

¾ cup crushed gingersnap
   cookies (about 15)

2 tablespoons packed
   brown sugar

2 tablespoons chopped fresh
   parsley

1 In 3½- to 4-quart slow cooker, mix beef, onions, broth, vinegar and bay leaves.

2 Cover; cook on Low heat setting 7 to 9 hours.

3 About 15 minutes before serving, cook noodles as directed on package. Remove bay leaves from beef mixture. Stir in crushed cookies and brown sugar. Cover; cook on Low heat setting 15 minutes longer or until mixture is bubbly and thickened. Serve beef mixture over noodles; sprinkle with parsley.

1 Serving: Calories 590; Total Fat 21g (Saturated Fat 7g, Trans Fat 1.5g); Cholesterol 140mg; Sodium 360mg; Total Carbohydrate 59g (Dietary Fiber 2g); Protein 39g **Exchanges:** 3 Starch, 1 Other Carbohydrate, 4 Lean Meat, 1½ Fat **Carbohydrate Choices:** 4

Pigs in Blankets

12 sandwiches • Prep Time: 15 Minutes • Start to Finish: 30 Minutes

2 cups all-purpose flour

2 teaspoons baking powder

½ teaspoon salt

¼ cup cold shortening

¾ cup milk

12 hot dogs or frankfurters

Mustard and ketchup, if desired

1 Heat oven to 425°F. In medium bowl, mix flour, baking powder and salt. Cut in shortening, using pastry blender or fork, until mixture looks like fine crumbs. Stir in milk until mixture leaves side of bowl (dough will be soft).

2 Place dough on floured surface. Knead lightly 10 times. Roll dough into a 16x9-inch rectangle, ¼-inch thick; cut into 12 (3x4-inch) rectangles. Place hot dog on one long edge of dough; roll up. Pinch long edges to seal. Place 2 inches apart on ungreased cookie sheet.

3 Bake 15 to 18 minutes or until dough is golden brown. Serve with mustard and ketchup.

1 Sandwich: Calories 260; Total Fat 18g (Saturated Fat 6g, Trans Fat 0g); Cholesterol 25mg; Sodium 720mg; Total Carbohydrate 18g (Dietary Fiber 0g); Protein 7g **Exchanges:** 1 Other Carbohydrate, 1 High-Fat Meat, 2 Fat **Carbohydrate Choices:** 1

CROWN ROAST OF PORK

16 servings • Prep Time: 35 Minutes • Start to Finish: 4 Hours 15 Minutes

PORK

1 pork crown roast (8 to 10 lb), 16 ribs

2 teaspoons salt

1 teaspoon pepper

MUSHROOM STUFFING

⅔ cup butter

2 medium stalks celery, chopped (1 cup)

1 medium onion, finely chopped (½ cup)

1 lb fresh mushrooms, sliced (6 cups)

8 cups unseasoned croutons

1 tablespoon chopped fresh or 1 teaspoon dried sage, thyme or marjoram

1 teaspoon poultry seasoning

1 teaspoon salt

½ teaspoon pepper

1 Heat oven to 325°F. Sprinkle pork with salt and pepper. Place pork with bone ends up on rack in shallow roasting pan. Wrap bone ends in foil to prevent excessive browning. Insert ovenproof meat thermometer so tip is in thickest part of pork and does not touch bone or rest in fat. Place small heatproof bowl or crumpled foil in crown to hold shape of roast evenly. Do not add water.

2 Roast uncovered 2 hours 40 minutes to 3 hours 20 minutes.

3 In 4-quart Dutch oven or large saucepan, melt butter over medium heat. Cook celery, onion and mushrooms in butter about 3 minutes, stirring occasionally, until tender. Stir in half of the croutons. Cook, stirring frequently, until evenly mixed and croutons are softened. Stir in remaining croutons and ingredients.

4 About 1 hour before pork is done, remove bowl and fill center of crown with stuffing. Cover stuffing with foil for first 30 minutes.

5 Remove pork from oven when thermometer reads 145°F; cover with tent of foil and let stand 15 to 20 minutes. Remove foil wrapping from bone ends. To serve, spoon stuffing into bowl and cut pork between ribs.

1 Serving: Calories 360; Total Fat 20g (Saturated Fat 8g, Trans Fat 0.5g); Cholesterol 110mg; Sodium 660mg; Total Carbohydrate 13g (Dietary Fiber 1g); Protein 34g **Exchanges:** 1 Starch, 4½ Lean Meat, 1 Fat **Carbohydrate Choices:** 1

Scalloped Potatoes with Ham

6 servings (1 cup each) • Prep Time: 50 Minutes • Start to Finish: 50 Minutes

2 tablespoons butter

1 clove garlic, finely chopped

2 lb Yukon gold or round red potatoes (about 4 medium), peeled, thinly sliced

½ lb fully cooked ham, cut into ½-inch pieces (about 2 cups)

1 cup shredded American-Cheddar cheese blend (4 oz)

3 tablespoons all-purpose flour

¼ teaspoon pepper

2 cups half-and-half

1 In 4-quart Dutch oven or large saucepan, melt butter over medium heat. Cook garlic in butter 1 minute, stirring occasionally, until softened. Remove from heat. Stir in potatoes, ham, cheese, flour and pepper.

2 Pour half-and-half over potato mixture. Heat to boiling over medium-high heat; reduce heat to low. Cover; simmer about 30 minutes, stirring occasionally, until potatoes are tender.

1 Serving: Calories 430; Total Fat 24g (Saturated Fat 13g, Trans Fat 0.5g); Cholesterol 85mg; Sodium 850mg; Total Carbohydrate 34g (Dietary Fiber 3g); Protein 20g **Exchanges:** 2 Starch, 2 Medium-Fat Meat, 2½ Fat **Carbohydrate Choices:** 2

Tuna-Noodle Casserole

6 servings • Prep Time: 20 Minutes • Start to Finish: 50 Minutes

1¼ cups uncooked medium egg noodles, medium pasta shells or elbow macaroni (3 to 4 oz)

2 tablespoons butter

2 tablespoons all-purpose flour

¾ teaspoon salt

2 cups milk

1 cup shredded American or pasteurized prepared cheese product sharp Cheddar cheese (4 oz)

1 cup frozen sweet peas, thawed*

1 can (12 oz) tuna in water, drained

⅔ cup dry bread crumbs**

1 tablespoon butter, melted

1. Heat oven to 350°F. Cook and drain noodles as directed on package.

2. Meanwhile, in 1½-quart saucepan, melt 2 tablespoons butter over low heat. Stir in flour and salt. Cook over medium heat, stirring constantly, until smooth and bubbly; remove from heat. Gradually stir in milk. Heat to boiling, stirring constantly. Boil and stir 1 minute. Stir in cheese until melted. Add noodles, peas and tuna; mix well.

3. Spoon into ungreased 2-quart casserole. Cover; bake about 25 to 30 minutes or until hot and bubbly.

4. In small bowl, mix bread crumbs and 1 tablespoon melted butter. Sprinkle over casserole. Bake uncovered about 5 to 10 minutes longer or until topping is toasted.

*You can substitute 2 cups fresh broccoli florets, cooked until crisp-tender and drained, for the peas. Or use frozen broccoli florets, thawed and drained (do not cook).

**You can substitute 1 cup broken or crushed regular or sour cream and onion-flavored potato chips for the bread crumbs. Omit butter.

1 Serving: Calories 380; Total Fat 15g (Saturated Fat 8g, Trans Fat 0.5g); Cholesterol 55mg; Sodium 910mg; Total Carbohydrate 37g (Dietary Fiber 3g); Protein 25g **Exchanges:** 2 Starch, 1 Vegetable, 2 Medium-Fat Meat, 1 Fat **Carbohydrate Choices:** 2½

Manhattan Clam Chowder

4 servings (about 1⅓ cups each) • Prep Time: 20 Minutes • Start to Finish: 35 Minutes

¼ cup chopped bacon or salt pork

1 small onion, finely chopped (⅓ cup)

2 cans (6.5 oz each) minced or chopped clams, undrained*

2 medium potatoes, peeled, diced (2 cups)

⅓ cup chopped celery

1 cup water

1 can (14.5 oz) whole tomatoes, undrained

2 teaspoons chopped fresh parsley

1 teaspoon chopped fresh or ¼ teaspoon dried thyme

¼ teaspoon salt

⅛ teaspoon pepper

1 In 2-quart saucepan, cook bacon and onion over medium heat 8 to 10 minutes, stirring occasionally, until bacon is crisp and onion is tender; drain.

2 Stir in clams, potatoes, celery and water. Heat to boiling; reduce heat. Cover and simmer about 15 minutes or until potatoes are tender.

3 Stir in remaining ingredients, breaking up tomatoes. Heat until hot, stirring occasionally.

*A pint shucked fresh clams with their liquid can be substituted for the canned clams. Chop the clams and stir in with the potatoes in Step 2.

1 Serving: Calories 230; Total Fat 3g (Saturated Fat 0.5g, Trans Fat 0g); Cholesterol 65mg; Sodium 450mg; Total Carbohydrate 23g (Dietary Fiber 3g); Protein 26g **Exchanges:** 1 Starch, 2 Vegetable, 3 Very Lean Meat **Carbohydrate Choices:** 1½

Cooks in Rhode Island in the late 1800s liked to throw tomatoes into clam chowder. Sometime in the mid-20th century, their creation became known as Manhattan clam chowder. It resembles New England clam chowder but is made with tomatoes instead of milk or cream.

LOBSTER NEWBURG

6 servings • Prep Time: 25 Minutes • Start to Finish: 25 Minutes

¼ cup butter

3 tablespoons all-purpose flour

½ teaspoon salt

½ teaspoon ground mustard

¼ teaspoon pepper

2 cups plus 2 tablespoons milk

2 cups cut up cooked lobster

2 tablespoons dry sherry or apple juice

6 cups hot cooked rice

Fresh parsley and additional pepper, if desired

1 In 3-quart saucepan, melt butter over medium heat. Stir in flour, salt, mustard and pepper. Cook, stirring constantly, until smooth and bubbly; remove from heat.

2 Stir in 2 cups of the milk. Heat to boiling, stirring constantly. Boil and stir 1 minute. Stir in lobster and sherry; heat through. (If sauce seems too thick, add remaining milk, 1 tablespoon at a time, until desired consistency is reached.) Serve over rice. Garnish with parsley and additional pepper.

1 Serving: Calories 170; Total Fat 2.5g (Saturated Fat 0g, Trans Fat 0g); Cholesterol 0mg; Sodium 1200mg; Total Carbohydrate 31g (Dietary Fiber 6g); Protein 6g **Exchanges:** 1 Starch, 1 Other Carbohydrate, ½ Fat **Carbohydrate Choices:** 2

Cheese Sandwich Loaf

12 servings • Prep Time: 1 Hour • Start to Finish: 4 Hours

RED FILLING

¼ cup finely chopped cooked ham

3 slices cooked bacon, crumbled

¼ cup sliced pimientos, drained, chopped

2 tablespoons mayonnaise

YELLOW FILLING

4 hard-cooked egg yolks, mashed

2 tablespoons mayonnaise

WHITE FILLING

2 oz cream cheese, softened

½ cup finely chopped peeled cucumber, well drained

1 tablespoon mayonnaise

GREEN FILLING

⅓ cup finely chopped sweet pickles, well drained

¼ cup finely chopped fresh watercress or parsley

3 tablespoons mayonnaise

LOAF

1 loaf (16 oz) unsliced sandwich bread

2 tablespoons butter, softened

2 packages (8 oz each) cream cheese, softened

¼ cup milk

Additional watercress, if desired

1 Mix each filling separately in small bowls. Using serrated knife, slice crusts from bread loaf. Cut loaf lengthwise to make 5 long slices.

2 Spread top of each slice with butter. Spread one filling on the bottom layer of bread. Top with one bread slice and spread one filling on top of bread. Repeat layers until all filling and bread are used. In medium bowl, mix cream cheese and milk until well blended. Spread cream cheese on outside of loaf, smoothing it as you spread.

3 Cover and refrigerate 3 hours or until firm. To serve, cut into ¾-inch slices. Garnish with additional watercress.

1 Serving: Calories 360; Total Fat 27g (Saturated Fat 12g, Trans Fat 0.5g); Cholesterol 115mg; Sodium 520mg; Total Carbohydrate 22g (Dietary Fiber 1g); Protein 8g **Exchanges:** 1 Starch, ½ Other Carbohydrate, ½ Medium-Fat Meat, 5 Fat **Carbohydrate Choices:** 1½

BETTY'S KITCHEN TIP

Use any of the ingredients in the pretty loaf to garnish the top of the loaf. Sweet pickles, pimiento, cucumber or watercress are a few suggestions.

Salmon Loaf

8 servings • Prep Time: 15 Minutes • Start to Finish: 1 Hour

2 cans (14.75 oz each) salmon, drained, flaked and liquid reserved

2 eggs

About 1 cup milk

3 cups coarse cracker crumbs

¼ cup chopped green onions (3 medium)

2 tablespoons lemon juice

¼ teaspoon salt

¼ teaspoon pepper

Lemon wedges, if desired

1 Heat oven to 350°F. Grease 9x5-inch loaf pan. In large bowl, mix salmon and eggs until blended. Add enough milk to reserved salmon liquid to measure 1½ cups. Stir liquid mixture and remaining ingredients except lemon wedges into salmon mixture. Spoon and spread evenly into pan.

2 Bake 40 to 50 minutes or until center is set. Garnish with lemon wedges.

1 Serving: Calories 260; Total Fat 9g (Saturated Fat 2.5g, Trans Fat 0g); Cholesterol 85mg; Sodium 690mg; Total Carbohydrate 22g (Dietary Fiber 1g); Protein 23g **Exchanges:** 1 Starch, ½ Other Carbohydrate, 3 Lean Meat **Carbohydrate Choices:** 1½

Classic Cheese Soufflé

4 servings • Prep Time: 25 Minutes • Start to Finish: 1 Hour 25 Minutes

¼ cup butter

¼ cup all-purpose flour

½ teaspoon salt

¼ teaspoon ground mustard

Dash cayenne

1 cup milk

1 cup shredded Cheddar cheese (4 oz)

3 eggs, separated

¼ teaspoon cream of tartar

1 Heat oven to 350°F. Butter 1-quart soufflé dish or casserole. Make a 4-inch-wide band of triple-thickness foil 2 inches longer than circumference of dish. Butter one side of foil. Secure foil band, buttered side in, around top edge of dish.

2 In 2-quart saucepan, melt ¼ cup butter over medium heat. Stir in flour, salt, mustard and cayenne. Cook over medium heat, stirring constantly, until smooth and bubbly; remove from heat. Stir in milk. Heat to boiling, stirring constantly. Boil and stir 1 minute. Stir in cheese until melted; remove from heat.

3 In medium bowl, beat egg whites and cream of tartar with electric mixer on high speed until stiff but not dry; set aside. In small bowl, beat egg yolks on high speed about 3 minutes or until very thick and lemon colored; stir into cheese mixture. Stir about one-fourth of the egg whites into cheese mixture. Fold cheese mixture into remaining egg whites. Carefully pour into soufflé dish.

4 Bake 50 to 60 minutes or until knife inserted halfway between center and edge comes out clean. Carefully remove foil band. Serve immediately by quickly dividing soufflé into sections with two forks.

1 Serving: Calories 330; Total Fat 26g (Saturated Fat 14g, Trans Fat 1g); Cholesterol 225mg; Sodium 620mg; Total Carbohydrate 10g (Dietary Fiber 0g); Protein 15g **Exchanges:** ½ Low-Fat Milk, 1½ High-Fat Meat, 3 Fat **Carbohydrate Choices:** ½

A versatile recipe from the 1956 Betty Crocker Picture Cook Book, this pretty gold and white dish is perfect for brunch and is a delicious way to make use of leftover hard-boiled eggs.

Eggs à la Goldenrod

4 servings • Prep Time: 30 Minutes • Start to Finish: 30 Minutes

4 hard-cooked eggs

2 tablespoons butter

2 tablespoons all-purpose flour

¼ teaspoon salt

⅛ teaspoon pepper

1 cup milk

4 to 6 slices buttered toast, chopped or torn into bite-size pieces

Additional pepper, if desired

1 Peel eggs; separate whites from yolks. Chop whites into bite-size pieces. In small bowl, mash yolks with fork or press through fine strainer. Set aside.

2 In 1-quart saucepan, melt butter over low heat. With whisk, beat in flour, salt and pepper. Cook over low heat, stirring, until mixture is smooth and bubbly. Remove sauce from heat. Stir in milk.

3 Return sauce to heat; heat to boiling, stirring constantly. Boil 1 minute or until sauce thickens slightly. Remove from heat. Fold chopped egg whites into white sauce.

4 To serve, arrange buttered toast pieces on 4 serving plates. Pour creamed eggs over buttered toast pieces; sprinkle with yolks. Sprinkle with additional pepper.

1 Serving: Calories 280; Total Fat 17g (Saturated Fat 9g, Trans Fat 0g); Cholesterol 215mg; Sodium 460mg; Total Carbohydrate 21g (Dietary Fiber 1g); Protein 12g **Exchanges:** 1 Starch, ½ Other Carbohydrate, 1 Medium-Fat Meat, 2½ Fat **Carbohydrate Choices:** 1½

EGGS À LA GOLDENROD
*Pretty gold and white main dish ready for luncheon.
Creamed Eggs with whites and some of yolks in the White Sauce,
poured over buttered toast . . . . . . sieved yolks over top.*

LUMBERJACK MACARONI

4 servings • Prep Time: 20 Minutes • Start to Finish: 20 Minutes

2 cups uncooked elbow macaroni (8 oz)

2 cups diced process cheese spread (8 oz)

½ cup butter, melted

¼ cup chili sauce

1 to 2 tablespoons Worcestershire sauce

⅛ teaspoon pepper

1 Cook and drain macaroni as directed on package; return macaroni to saucepan.

2 Stir in remaining ingredients; cook and stir over medium heat until cheese is melted. Serve immediately.

1 Serving: Calories 680; Total Fat 39g (Saturated Fat 24g, Trans Fat 1.5g); Cholesterol 120mg; Sodium 1690mg; Total Carbohydrate 60g (Dietary Fiber 4g); Protein 22g **Exchanges:** 2½ Starch, 1½ Other Carbohydrate, 2 High-Fat Meat, 4½ Fat **Carbohydrate Choices:** 4

Baked Eggs

2 servings • Prep Time: 5 Minutes • Start to Finish: 25 Minutes

2   eggs
⅛   teaspoon salt
    Dash pepper
2   tablespoons milk or half-and-half
2   teaspoons butter

1 Heat oven to 325°F. Grease 2 (6-oz) custard cups with butter. Break 1 egg into each cup; sprinkle with salt and pepper. Top each with 1 tablespoon milk and 1 teaspoon butter.

2 Bake 15 to 18 minutes or until whites and yolks are firm, not runny.

1 Serving: Calories 120; Total Fat 9g (Saturated Fat 4.5g, Trans Fat 0g); Cholesterol 200mg; Sodium 250mg; Total Carbohydrate 1g (Dietary Fiber 0g); Protein 7g **Exchanges:** 1 Medium-Fat Meat, 1 Fat **Carbohydrate Choices:** 0

Welsh Rarebit (Welsh Rabbit)

6 servings • Prep Time: 15 Minutes • Start to Finish: 15 Minutes

4 cups finely shredded sharp Cheddar cheese (16 oz)

¾ cup half-and-half

½ teaspoon dry mustard

½ teaspoon Worcestershire sauce

Dash pepper

12 slices bread, toasted

Sliced green onions, paprika and additional pepper, if desired

1 Place cheese, half-and-half, mustard, Worcestershire sauce and pepper in medium saucepan. Heat over low heat, stirring constantly, about 10 minutes or until cheese is melted and mixture is smooth.

2 Serve cheese sauce over toast. Garnish with green onions, paprika and additional pepper.

1 Serving: Calories 500; Total Fat 31g (Saturated Fat 17g, Trans Fat 1g); Cholesterol 90mg; Sodium 800mg; Total Carbohydrate 31g (Dietary Fiber 2g); Protein 25g **Exchanges:** 2 Starch, 2½ High-Fat Meat, 2 Fat **Carbohydrate Choices:** 2

BLAST FROM THE PAST:

(*Betty Crocker Picture Cook Book*, 1950)
Original "All You Have to Do" Tip

To make Welsh Rarebit de Luxe: use ginger ale in place of cream.

Cantonese Chicken Chop Suey

4 servings • Prep Time: 10 Minutes • Start to Finish: 35 Minutes

1 cup uncooked long-grain rice

1 lb boneless skinless chicken breast halves

¼ teaspoon salt

1 bag (12 oz) fresh stir-fry vegetables (about 3 cups)

½ cup water

½ cup classic-style stir-fry sauce

1 tablespoon honey

2 cups chow mein noodles

¼ cup cashew pieces

1 Cook rice as directed on package.

2 While rice is cooking, cut chicken into ½-inch pieces. Spray 12-inch nonstick skillet with cooking spray; heat over medium-high heat. Add chicken; sprinkle with salt. Stir-fry 4 to 6 minutes or until brown.

3 Add vegetables and water to skillet. Heat to boiling; reduce heat to medium. Cover and cook 5 to 7 minutes, stirring occasionally, until vegetables are crisp-tender. Stir in stir-fry sauce and honey; heat through.

4 Divide rice and noodles among bowls. Top with chicken mixture. Sprinkle with cashews.

1 Serving: Calories 580; Total Fat 17g (Saturated Fat 3g, Trans Fat 0g); Cholesterol 70mg; Sodium 2240mg; Total Carbohydrate 75g (Dietary Fiber 5g); Protein 37g **Exchanges:** 5 Starch, 3 Lean Meat, 1 Fat **Carbohydrate Choices:** 5

BETTY'S KITCHEN TIP

Make your own stir-fry vegetable combination by mixing 1½ cups sliced celery, 1¼ cups sliced carrots, ¾ cup snow (Chinese) pea pods and ½ cup coarsely chopped onion.

Breads & Coffee Cakes

Cherry Swirl Coffee Cake

18 servings • Prep Time: 20 Minutes • Start to Finish: 45 Minutes

COFFEE CAKE

4 cups Original Bisquick mix

½ cup granulated sugar

¼ cup butter, melted

½ cup milk

1 teaspoon vanilla

1 teaspoon almond extract

3 eggs

1 can (21 oz) cherry pie filling

GLAZE

1 cup powdered sugar

1 to 2 tablespoons milk

1 Heat oven to 350°F. Grease bottom and sides of one 15x10x1-inch pan or two 9-inch square pans with shortening or cooking spray. In large bowl, stir together all coffee cake ingredients except pie filling; beat vigorously with spoon 30 seconds.

2 Spread two-thirds of the batter (about 2½ cups) in 15x10-inch pan or one-third of the batter (about 1¼ cups) in each square pan. Spread pie filling over batter (filling may not cover batter completely). Drop remaining batter by tablespoonfuls onto pie filling.

3 Bake 20 to 25 minutes or until light brown. Meanwhile, in small bowl, stir together glaze ingredients until smooth and thin enough to drizzle. Drizzle glaze over warm coffee cake. Serve warm or cool.

1 Serving: Calories 240; Total Fat 8g (Saturated Fat 3g, Trans Fat 1g); Cholesterol 45mg; Sodium 360mg; Total Carbohydrate 39g (Dietary Fiber 1g); Protein 4g **Exchanges:** 1 Starch, 1½ Other Carbohydrate, 1½ Fat **Carbohydrate Choices:** 2½

Puffy Oven Pancake

4 servings • Prep Time: 10 Minutes • Start to Finish: 40 Minutes

2 tablespoons butter

2 eggs

½ cup all-purpose flour

¼ teaspoon salt

½ cup milk

Lemon juice and powdered sugar or cut-up fruit, if desired

1 Heat oven to 400°F. In 9-inch glass pie plate, melt butter in oven; brush butter over bottom and sides of pie plate.

2 In medium bowl, beat eggs slightly with whisk. Stir in flour, salt and milk just until flour is moistened (do not overbeat or pancake may not puff). Pour into pie plate.

3 Bake 25 to 30 minutes or until puffy and deep golden brown. Serve immediately, sprinkled with lemon juice and powdered sugar or topped with fruit.

1 Serving: Calories 160; Total Fat 9g (Saturated Fat 5g, Trans Fat 0g); Cholesterol 125mg; Sodium 230mg; Total Carbohydrate 14g (Dietary Fiber 0g); Protein 5g **Exchanges:** 1 Starch, 2 Fat **Carbohydrate Choices:** 1

Apple Oven Pancake Make pancake as directed, except sprinkle 2 tablespoons packed brown sugar and ¼ teaspoon ground cinnamon evenly over melted butter in pie plate. Arrange 1 cup thinly sliced peeled baking apple (1 medium) over sugar. Pour batter over apple. Bake 30 to 35 minutes. Immediately loosen edge of pancake and turn upside down onto heatproof serving plate.

Sweet Muffins

. . . .

12 muffins • Prep Time: 10 Minutes • Start to Finish: 30 Minutes

. . . .

1 egg

½ cup milk

¼ cup vegetable oil or melted butter

1½ cups all-purpose flour

½ cup sugar

2 teaspoons baking powder

½ teaspoon salt

1 Heat oven to 400°F. Grease bottoms only of 12 regular-size muffin cups with shortening or line with paper baking cups. In large bowl, beat egg slightly. Beat in milk and oil until blended.

2 Stir in flour, sugar, baking powder and salt all at once just until flour is moistened (batter will be lumpy). Spoon batter into muffin cups.

3 Bake 20 to 25 minutes or until golden brown. If baked in greased pan, let stand 5 minutes in pan, then remove from pan to wire rack. If baked in paper baking cups, remove immediately from pan to wire rack. Serve warm.

1 Muffin: Calories 140; Total Fat 5g (Saturated Fat 1g, Trans Fat 0g); Cholesterol 15mg; Sodium 190mg; Total Carbohydrate 21g (Dietary Fiber 0g); Protein 2g **Exchanges:** 1 Starch, ½ Other Carbohydrate, 1 Fat **Carbohydrate Choices:** 1½

Less Sweet Muffins For muffins that are less sweet, use 1 cup milk, 2 cups flour, ¼ cup sugar and 1 tablespoon baking powder.

Swedish Tea Ring

12 servings • Prep Time: 40 Minutes • Start to Finish: 3 Hours 15 Minutes

DOUGH

3½ to 4 cups all-purpose or bread flour

⅓ cup granulated sugar

1 teaspoon salt

2 envelopes (2¼ teaspoons each) regular active or fast-acting dry yeast

1 cup very warm milk (120°F to 130°F)

¼ cup butter, softened

1 egg

TEA RING

2 tablespoons butter, softened

½ cup packed brown sugar

2 teaspoons ground cinnamon

½ cup raisins

FROSTING

1 cup powdered sugar

1 tablespoon milk

½ teaspoon vanilla

Maraschino cherries, drained, if desired

1. In large bowl, mix 2 cups of the flour, granulated sugar, salt and yeast. Add warm milk, ¼ cup butter and egg. Beat with electric mixer on low speed 1 minute, scraping bowl frequently. Beat on medium speed 1 minute, scraping bowl frequently. Stir in enough remaining flour, ½ cup at a time, to make dough easy to handle.

2. Place dough on lightly floured surface. Knead about 5 minutes or until dough is smooth and springy. Grease large bowl with shortening. Place dough in bowl, turning dough to grease all sides. Cover bowl loosely with plastic wrap; let rise in warm place about 1 hour 30 minutes or until dough has doubled in size. Dough is ready if indentation remains when touched.

3. Grease cookie sheet. Gently push fist into dough to deflate. Roll dough into 15x9-inch rectangle on lightly floured surface. Spread with 2 tablespoons butter; sprinkle with brown sugar, cinnamon and raisins. Roll rectangle up, starting with 15-inch side. Pinch edge of dough to seal well. With sealed edge facing down, shape into ring on cookie sheet. Pinch ends together. With scissors, make cuts two-thirds of the way into ring at 1-inch intervals. Carefully turn each section to show filling. Cover loosely with plastic wrap; let rise in warm place about 30 minutes or until dough has doubled in size.

4. Heat oven to 350°F. Bake tea ring 25 to 30 minutes or until golden brown. Cool slightly. In small bowl, mix frosting ingredients except cherries until smooth; spread over warm tea ring. Decorate with cherries.

1 Serving: Calories 320; Total Fat 7g (Saturated Fat 4g, Trans Fat 0g); Cholesterol 15mg; Sodium 260mg; Total Carbohydrate 59g (Dietary Fiber 2g); Protein 5g **Exchanges:** 1 Starch, 3 Other Carbohydrate, 1½ Fat **Carbohydrate Choices:** 4

Danish Puff is a delicious contrast of textures, with its flaky layers and smooth glaze, making it a unique treat.

DANISH PUFF

10 servings • Prep Time: 20 Minutes • Start to Finish: 1 Hour 20 Minutes

PASTRY

1 cup all-purpose flour
½ cup butter, softened
2 tablespoons water

TOPPING

½ cup butter
1 cup water
1 teaspoon almond extract
1 cup all-purpose flour
3 eggs

CREAMY VANILLA GLAZE

1½ cups powdered sugar
2 tablespoons butter, softened
½ teaspoon vanilla
1 to 2 tablespoons warm water or milk
Sliced almonds, toasted*, if desired

1 Heat oven to 350°F. Place 1 cup flour in medium bowl. Cut in ½ cup softened butter, using pastry blender or fork, until particles are size of coarse crumbs. Sprinkle 2 tablespoons water over mixture; toss with fork.

2 Gather pastry into a ball; divide in half. Pat each half into 12x3-inch rectangle, about 3 inches apart on ungreased cookie sheet.

3 In 2-quart saucepan, heat ½ cup butter and 1 cup water to rolling boil; remove from heat. Quickly stir in almond extract and 1 cup flour. Stir vigorously over low heat about 1 minute or until mixture forms a ball; remove from heat. Add eggs; beat until smooth. Spread half of topping over each rectangle.

4 Bake about 1 hour or until topping is crisp and brown; remove from pan to cooling rack. Cool completely.

5 In medium bowl, mix all glaze ingredients except nuts until smooth and spreadable. Spread over top of pastry; sprinkle with almonds.

*To toast almonds, spread in ungreased shallow pan. Bake uncovered at 350°F for 6 to 10 minutes, stirring occasionally, until light brown.

1 Serving: Calories 380; Total Fat 23g (Saturated Fat 14g, Trans Fat 1g); Cholesterol 120mg; Sodium 170mg; Total Carbohydrate 38g (Dietary Fiber 0g); Protein 5g **Exchanges:** 1½ Starch, 1 Other Carbohydrate, 4½ Fat **Carbohydrate Choices:** 2½

BETTY'S KITCHEN TIP

You can serve this double-textured pastry as a bread or dessert. What an elegant addition to a brunch buffet table!

Raspberry Peek-a-Boos

12 muffins • Prep Time: 20 Minutes • Start to Finish: 40 Minutes

MUFFINS

- 1 cup fresh raspberries
- 4 tablespoons granulated sugar
- 1 teaspoon lemon juice
- ½ teaspoon ground nutmeg
- ½ teaspoon ground cinnamon
- 2 cups Original Bisquick mix
- ¼ cup butter, softened
- ⅔ cup milk

GLAZE

- 1 cup powdered sugar
- ½ teaspoon vanilla
  Pinch of salt
- 1 to 2 tablespoons milk

1 Heat oven to 400°F. Place paper baking cup in each of 12 regular-size muffin cups, or grease muffin cups. In small bowl, toss raspberries, 2 tablespoons of the granulated sugar, lemon juice, nutmeg and cinnamon. Set aside.

2 In medium bowl, combine Bisquick mix, remaining 2 tablespoons granulated sugar and butter. Add milk all at once; stir just until moistened.

3 Spread 1 tablespoon of dough in bottom of each muffin cup. Top each with 1 tablespoon raspberry mixture. Drop about 1 tablespoon dough onto berries.

4 Bake 13 to 15 minutes or until golden brown. Cool slightly; remove from muffin pans. Cool about 10 minutes.

5 Meanwhile, in small bowl, stir together glaze ingredients, adding milk 1 tablespoon at a time until drizzling consistency. Drizzle over muffins.

1 Muffin: Calories 190; Total Fat 7g (Saturated Fat 4g, Trans Fat 0g); Cholesterol 10mg; Sodium 290mg; Total Carbohydrate 28g (Dietary Fiber 0g); Protein 2g **Exchanges:** ½ Starch, 1½ Other Carbohydrate, 1½ Fat **Carbohydrate Choices:** 2

TIME FOR A TEA PARTY

Whether it's afternoon tea, with light, dainty sweets and treats, high tea or a children's bash, throwing a tea party can be a lot of fun without a lot of effort.

START WITH THE TEA

You may wish to serve one or two brewed teas or a pot of hot water with Orange Tea Mix (page 39) or a variety of tea bags, or depending on the time of year, a hot and cold option. Offer condiments such as lemon wedges, cream, honey and sugar. For a fun change of pace, offer rock candy sticks (available in specialty candy stores or online). Don't like tea? Try Frosty Citrus Punch (page 40) served in wineglasses, champagne glasses or mason jars. Add colorful straws or swizzle sticks.

CHOOSE PARTY FOODS

For late morning or early afternoon tea, light foods such as scones with jam and cookies such as Cherry Blinks (page 201) would be perfect. For something a little more filling, Cheese Sandwich Loaf (page 96) is a classic choice.

High tea is actually like a light presupper, so the food is usually heartier. Meats and cheeses or satisfying dishes such as Welsh Rarebit (page 104) may be served in addition to vegetables, potatoes and crackers.

Fancy and frilly is the name of the game when it comes to decorating. Offer trays of food at different heights for interest. Decorate with fresh flowers or strands of pearls. Small framed antique pictures can be a nice touch.

For a children's tea party, set up at a child-size table and chairs. Milk can be the tea. Offer stir-ins for their "tea," such as chocolate syrup, caramel syrup and malted milk powder.

Dress up with hats and gloves, if you like. Or have a box full of props for everyone to dress up in and take selfies, as a memento of the party. Thrift stores are a great place to find dresses, hats, gloves, jewelry and teacups to use in the photos. Lighten the formalness with small signs to hold in the photos, with assorted phrases on them, such as "Tea Time," "Happiness in a Cup" or "One Lump or Two?"

Applesauce Doughnuts

18 doughnuts • Prep Time: 40 Minutes • Start to Finish: 1 Hour 40 Minutes

3⅓ cups all-purpose flour

1 cup applesauce

¾ cup sugar

2 tablespoons shortening

1 tablespoon baking powder

1 teaspoon ground cinnamon

½ teaspoon salt

2 eggs

Vegetable oil

Cinnamon-sugar mixture, if desired

1 Beat 1⅓ cups of the flour and the remaining ingredients except oil and cinnamon-sugar in large bowl with electric mixer on low speed, scraping bowl constantly, until blended. Beat on medium speed 2 minutes, scraping bowl occasionally. Stir in remaining 2 cups flour. Cover and refrigerate about 1 hour or until dough stiffens.

2 In deep fryer or 3-quart saucepan, heat 2 to 3 inches oil to 375°F. Divide dough in half. Place half of the dough on well-floured cloth-covered surface; gently roll in flour to coat. Gently roll dough ⅜ inch thick. Cut with floured doughnut cutter. Repeat with remaining dough.

3 Fry doughnuts and holes in oil, 2 or 3 doughnuts at a time, sliding in with a wide spatula and turning as they rise to surface. Fry 1 to 1½ minutes on each side or until golden brown. Remove from oil with slotted spoon; drain on paper towels. Sprinkle hot doughnuts with cinnamon-sugar.

1 Doughnut: Calories 230; Total Fat 11g (Saturated Fat 2g, Trans Fat 0g); Cholesterol 20mg; Sodium 150mg; Total Carbohydrate 29g (Dietary Fiber 1g); Protein 3g **Exchanges:** 1 Starch, 1 Other Carbohydrate, 2 Fat **Carbohydrate Choices:** 2

This quotation appeared with the recipe in the 1961 edition of the cookbook: "When Florida hunters sat around their camp fish-fries, their dogs would whine for the good-smelling food. The men would toss leftover corn patties to them, calling, 'Hush, puppies.' Satisfied, the dogs hushed."

HUSH PUPPIES

24 hush puppies • Prep Time: 45 Minutes • Start to Finish: 45 Minutes

1½ cups yellow cornmeal

1½ cups water

⅓ cup milk

1 tablespoon vegetable oil, plus more for frying

2 teaspoons grated onion

2 eggs

1 cup all-purpose flour

1 tablespoon baking powder

1 teaspoon salt

1 teaspoon sugar

1 In 2-quart saucepan, cook cornmeal and water over medium heat 5 to 6 minutes, stirring constantly, until mixture is stiff and begins to form a ball. Remove from heat. Stir in milk, 1 tablespoon oil and onion until well blended.

2 In medium bowl, beat eggs slightly. Beat in flour, baking powder, salt and sugar. Add to cornmeal mixture; beat until smooth.

3 In deep fryer or 4-quart Dutch oven, heat 1 to 2 inches oil to 375°F. Drop batter by teaspoonfuls into hot oil. Cook 5 to 7 minutes or until golden brown. Drain on paper towels.

1 Hush Puppy: Calories 110; Total Fat 6g (Saturated Fat 1g, Trans Fat 0g); Cholesterol 15mg; Sodium 170mg; Total Carbohydrate 12g (Dietary Fiber 0g); Protein 2g **Exchanges:** 1 Starch, 1 Fat **Carbohydrate Choices:** 1

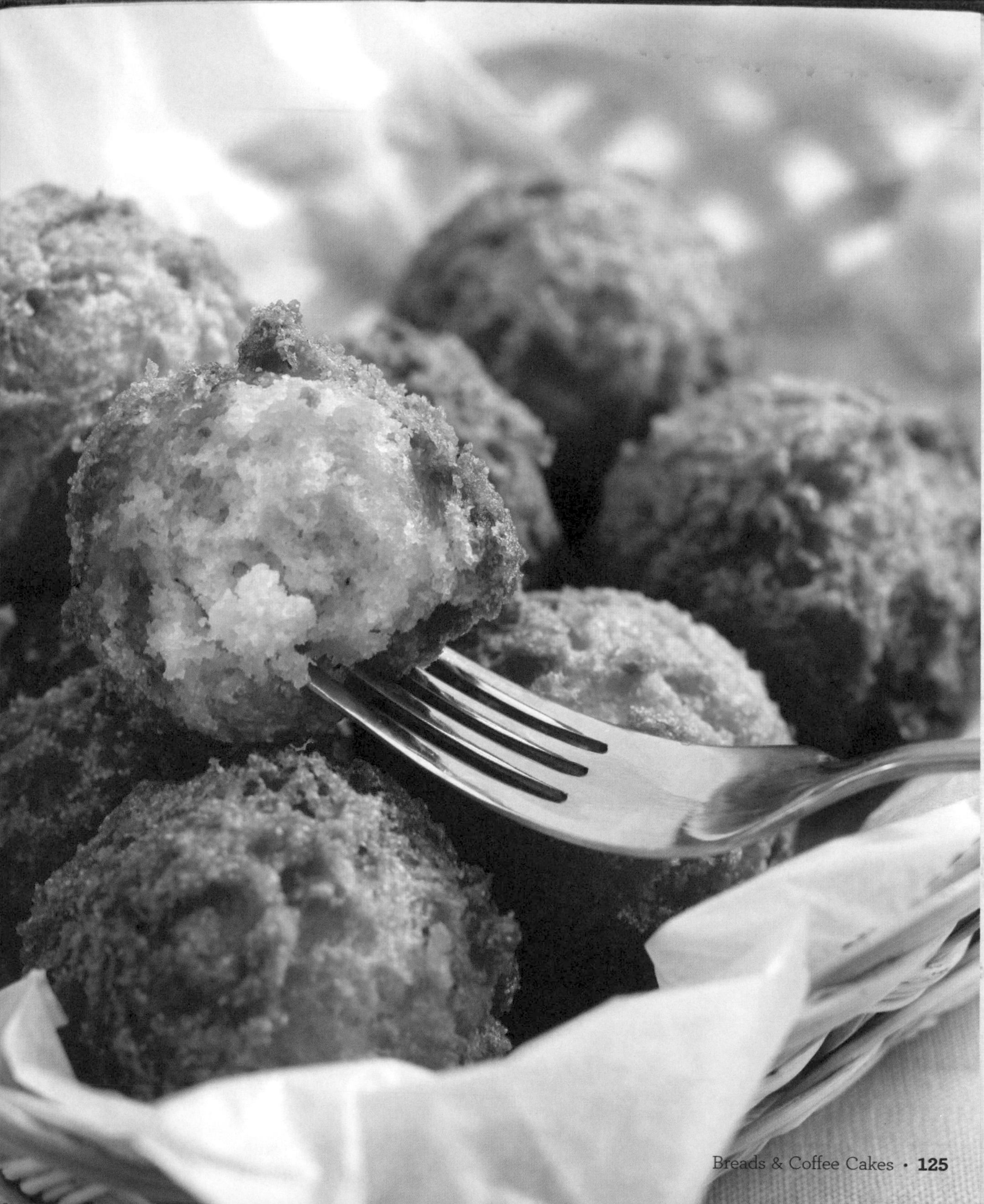

Stir 'n Roll Biscuits

12 biscuits • Prep Time: 15 Minutes • Start to Finish: 30 Minutes

2   cups all-purpose flour
2   teaspoons baking powder
1   teaspoon salt
⅓   cup vegetable oil
⅔   cup milk

1   Heat oven to 450°F. In medium bowl, mix flour, baking powder and salt. Add oil and milk; stir with spoon until mixture begins to leave sides of bowl.

2   Place dough on lightly floured surface. Knead lightly 10 times. Roll dough ½ inch thick. Cut with floured 2-inch round biscuit cutter. Place biscuits 2 inches apart on ungreased cookie sheet.

3   Bake 10 to 12 minutes or until golden brown. Remove from cookie sheet to wire rack. Serve warm.

1 Biscuit: Calories 140; Total Fat 7g (Saturated Fat 1g, Trans Fat 0g); Cholesterol 0mg; Sodium 280mg; Total Carbohydrate 17g (Dietary Fiber 0g); Protein 2g
Exchanges: 1 Starch, 1½ Fat **Carbohydrate Choices:** 1

Buttermilk Biscuits Use buttermilk instead of milk, reduce baking powder to 2 teaspoons and add ¼ teaspoon baking soda.

For larger biscuits, cut dough using 3-inch round biscuit cutter into 5 biscuits. Bake 11 to 13 minutes.

Mixer Batter Buns

30 buns • Prep Time: 15 Minutes • Start to Finish: 1 Hour 15 Minutes

1¼ cups warm water (110°F to 115°F)

2 envelopes (2¼ teaspoons each) active dry yeast

¼ cup sugar

1 teaspoon salt

½ cup butter, softened

2 eggs

3¼ cups all-purpose flour

1 Grease 30 regular-size muffin cups. Pour warm water into large bowl; sprinkle yeast on top. Stir until dissolved. Stir in sugar, salt, butter, eggs and 2 cups of the flour. Beat on low speed of mixer 1 minute. Beat on medium speed 2 minutes, scraping bowl frequently. Using spoon, beat in remaining 1¼ cups flour until batter is smooth. Spoon evenly into muffin cups.

2 Cover loosely with plastic wrap; let rise in warm place 30 to 40 minutes or until batter reaches top of muffin cups. Heat oven to 375°F.

3 Uncover muffin cups. Bake buns 18 to 20 minutes or until golden brown.

1 Bun: Calories 90; Total Fat 3.5g (Saturated Fat 2g, Trans Fat 0g); Cholesterol 20mg; Sodium 110mg; Total Carbohydrate 12g (Dietary Fiber 0g); Protein 2g
Exchanges: 1 Starch, ½ Fat **Carbohydrate Choices:** 1

Cinnamon-Butter Buns Bake buns as directed. In small bowl, mix ½ cup sugar and 1 teaspoon ground cinnamon. After baking, roll warm buns in ¼ cup melted butter. Coat with cinnamon-sugar mixture; place on wire rack.

Refrigerator Potato Rolls

48 rolls • Prep Time: 20 Minutes • Start to Finish: 10 Hours 15 Minutes

1½ cups warm water (120°F to 130°F)

1 envelope (2¼ teaspoons) active dry yeast

⅔ cup sugar

1 teaspoon salt

⅔ cup butter, softened

2 eggs

1 cup lukewarm mashed potatoes

7 to 7½ cups all-purpose flour

1 In large bowl, combine water and yeast; stir until yeast is dissolved. Stir in sugar, salt, butter, eggs, potatoes and 4 cups of the flour. Beat until smooth. Stir in enough remaining flour until dough pulls away from sides of bowl.

2 Place dough on lightly floured surface. Knead 5 minutes or until smooth and elastic. Spray large bowl with cooking spray. Place dough in bowl, turning to grease all sides. Cover bowl loosely with plastic wrap; refrigerate at least 8 hours or up to 5 days.

3 Punch dough to remove air bubbles. Spray large cookie sheets with cooking spray. Divide dough into 4 equal pieces. Shape dough pieces into desired roll shape (see following page). Place rolls 2 inches apart on cookie sheets. Cover with plastic wrap; let rise in warm place 1½ hours or until doubled in size.

4 Heat oven to 400°F. Bake rolls 15 to 20 minutes or until golden brown.

1 Roll: Calories 110; Total Fat 3g (Saturated Fat 1.5g, Trans Fat 0g); Cholesterol 15mg; Sodium 75mg; Total Carbohydrate 18g (Dietary Fiber 0g); Protein 2g **Exchanges:** 1 Starch, ½ Fat **Carbohydrate Choices:** 1

ROLL SHAPES

Cloverleaf Rolls Spray 12 regular-size muffin cups with cooking spray. Divide dough into 1-inch balls. Place 3 balls in each muffin cup. Brush with butter. Makes 12 rolls.

Crescent Rolls Spray large cookie sheets with cooking spray. Roll dough into 12-inch circle, about ¼ inch thick. Spread with 2 tablespoons softened butter. Cut into 12 wedges. Roll up starting at rounded edge. Place rolls, point side down, on cookie sheet. Curve slightly. Brush with butter. Makes 12 rolls.

Fan Tan Rolls Spray 12 regular-size muffin cups with cooking spray. Roll dough into 13x9-inch rectangle. Spread with 2 tablespoons softened butter. Cut crosswise into 6 strips, 1½ inches wide. Stack strips evenly; cut into 12 pieces, about 1 inch wide. Place cut-side down in muffin cups. Brush with butter. Makes 12 rolls.

Four-Leaf Clover Rolls Spray 12 regular-size muffin cups with cooking spray. Shape dough into 12 (2-inch) balls. Place 1 ball in each muffin cup. With scissors, snip each ball in half, then into quarters. Brush with butter. Makes 12 rolls.

DINNER ROLLS

15 rolls • Prep Time: 30 Minutes • Start to Finish: 2 Hours 15 Minutes

3½ to 3¾ cups all-purpose or bread flour

¼ cup sugar

¼ cup butter, softened

1 teaspoon salt

1 envelope (2¼ teaspoons) regular active or fast-acting dry yeast

½ cup very warm water (120°F to 130°F)

½ cup very warm milk (120°F to 130°F)

1 egg

Melted butter, if desired

1 In large bowl, stir together 2 cups of the flour, sugar, ¼ cup butter, salt and yeast until well mixed. Add warm water, warm milk and egg. Beat with electric mixer on low speed 1 minute, scraping bowl frequently. Beat on medium speed 1 minute, scraping bowl frequently. Stir in enough remaining flour, ¼ cup at a time, to make dough easy to handle.

2 Place dough on lightly floured surface. Knead about 5 minutes or until dough is smooth and springy. Grease large bowl with shortening. Place dough in bowl, turning dough to grease all sides. Cover bowl loosely with plastic wrap and let rise in warm place about 1 hour or until dough has doubled in size. Dough is ready if indentation remains when touched.

3 Grease bottom and sides of 13x9-inch pan with shortening or cooking spray. Gently push fist into dough to deflate. Divide dough into 15 equal pieces. Shape each piece into a ball; place in pan. Brush with melted butter. Cover loosely with plastic wrap and let rise in warm place about 30 minutes or until dough has doubled in size.

4 Heat oven to 375°F. Uncover rolls. Bake 12 to 15 minutes or until golden brown. Serve warm if desired.

1 Roll: Calories 160; Total Fat 4g (Saturated Fat 2g, Trans Fat 0g); Cholesterol 25mg; Sodium 190mg; Total Carbohydrate 26g (Dietary Fiber 1g); Protein 4g
Exchanges: 2 Starch **Carbohydrate Choices:** 2

Make-Ahead Directions After placing rolls in pan, cover tightly with foil and refrigerate 4 to 24 hours. About 2 hours before baking, remove from refrigerator; remove foil and cover loosely with plastic wrap. Let rise in warm place until dough has doubled in size. If some rising has occurred in the refrigerator, rising time may be less than 2 hours. Bake as directed.

Cloverleaf Rolls Grease 24 regular-size muffin cups with shortening or cooking spray. Make dough as directed—except after pushing fist into dough, divide dough into 72 equal pieces. (To divide, cut dough in half, then continue cutting pieces in half until there are 72 pieces.) Shape each piece into a ball. Place 3 balls in each muffin cup. Brush with melted butter. Cover loosely with plastic wrap and let rise in warm place about 30 minutes or until dough has doubled in size. Bake as directed. Makes 24 rolls.

Crescent Rolls Grease cookie sheet with shortening or cooking spray. Make dough as directed—except after pushing fist into dough, cut dough in half. Roll each half into 12-inch round on floured surface. Spread with softened butter. Cut each circle into 16 wedges. Roll up each wedge, beginning at rounded edge. Place rolls, with points underneath, on cookie sheet and curve slightly. Brush with melted butter. Cover loosely with plastic wrap and let rise in warm place about 30 minutes or until dough has doubled in size. Bake as directed. Makes 32 rolls.

BLAST FROM THE PAST:

(*Betty Crocker Picture Cook Book*, 1950)
Original "All You Have to Do" Tip

To reheat breads or rolls: place in paper bag, sprinkle bag with water, heat in 400°F oven 10 minutes, or heat in bun warmer on top of stove.

POPOVERS

6 popovers • Prep Time: 10 Minutes • Start to Finish: 45 Minutes

2 eggs
1 cup all-purpose flour
1 cup milk
½ teaspoon salt

1 Heat oven to 450°F. Generously grease 6-cup popover pan with shortening. Heat popover pan in oven 5 minutes.

2 Meanwhile, in medium bowl, beat eggs slightly with fork or whisk. Beat in remaining ingredients just until smooth (do not overbeat or popovers may not puff as high). Fill cups about half full.

3 Bake 20 minutes. Reduce oven temperature to 325°F. Bake 10 to 15 minutes longer or until deep golden brown. Immediately remove from cups. Serve hot.

1 Popover: Calories 120; Total Fat 3g (Saturated Fat 1g, Trans Fat 0g); Cholesterol 75mg; Sodium 240mg; Total Carbohydrate 18g (Dietary Fiber 0g); Protein 6g **Exchanges:** 1 Starch, 1 Fat **Carbohydrate Choices:** 1

ANADAMA BREAD

1 loaf (16 slices) • Prep Time: 20 Minutes • Start to Finish: 2 Hours 45 Minutes

¾ cup boiling water

½ cup yellow cornmeal

3 tablespoons butter, softened

¼ cup light molasses

1 teaspoon salt

¼ cup warm water (120°F to 130°F)

1 envelope (2¼ teaspoons) active dry yeast

1 egg

2¾ cups all-purpose flour

1 tablespoon butter, melted

BLAST FROM THE PAST:

(*Betty Crocker Picture Cook Book*, 1950)

Original "All You Have to Do" Tip

To give the birds a treat: a feeding box for birds offers a pleasant way of using leftover bread crumbs, and gives delight to the family.

1 Grease 8- or 9-inch loaf pan; sprinkle with cornmeal. In large bowl, stir together boiling water, cornmeal, softened butter, molasses and salt until blended. Cool 5 minutes or until lukewarm. Pour water into small bowl and sprinkle yeast on top. Stir until dissolved.

2 Add yeast, egg and 1½ cups of the flour to cornmeal mixture. Beat with electric mixer on medium speed 2 minutes, scraping bowl frequently. Add remaining 1¼ cups flour; stir with spoon until well blended. Spoon and spread batter in pan.

3 Cover pan with plastic wrap. Let rise in warm place 1 hour 15 minutes to 1 hour 30 minutes or until batter reaches top of 8-inch pan or is 1 inch from top of 9-inch pan. Heat oven to 375°F.

4 Bake loaf 50 to 55 minutes or until it sounds hollow when tapped and is dark golden brown. Immediately remove from pan to wire rack. Brush warm loaf with melted butter.

1 Slice: Calories 140; Total Fat 3.5g (Saturated Fat 2g, Trans Fat 0g); Cholesterol 20mg; Sodium 180mg; Total Carbohydrate 24g (Dietary Fiber 1g); Protein 3g **Exchanges:** 1 Starch, ½ Other Carbohydrate, ½ Fat **Carbohydrate Choices:** 1½

This recipe came to America from Bath, England, home of Sally Lunn. The distinctive feature is the shape, a tube pan. The texture is fluffy, porous and sponge-like.

SALLY LUNN

1 loaf (16 slices) • Prep Time: 30 Minutes • Start to Finish: 2 Hours 15 Minutes

½ cup very warm water (120°F to 130°F)

2 envelopes (2¼ teaspoons each) active dry yeast

5½ cups all-purpose flour

1½ cups very warm milk (120°F to 130°F)

¼ cup butter, cut into small pieces

2 tablespoons sugar

1 teaspoon salt

2 eggs

1 tablespoon butter, if desired

Softened butter and jam, if desired

1 In large bowl, mix warm water and yeast; stir until dissolved. Stir in all remaining ingredients except 1 tablespoon butter. Beat with spoon until dough pulls cleanly away from sides of bowl and is smooth. Cover bowl loosely with plastic wrap; let rise in warm place about 1 hour or until doubled in size.

2 Grease or spray 10-inch tube pan with cooking spray. Stir down dough with spoon. Pour evenly into pan. Cover with plastic wrap; let rise in warm place about 30 minutes or until dough is about 1 inch below top of pan. Heat oven to 350°F.

3 Bake loaf 45 to 50 minutes or until golden brown. Immediately remove from pan using knife to loosen edges if necessary; place on wire rack. Brush warm bread with 1 tablespoon butter. Serve warm or cool with softened butter and jam.

1 Slice: Calories 210; Total Fat 4.5g (Saturated Fat 2.5g, Trans Fat 0g); Cholesterol 35mg; Sodium 190mg; Total Carbohydrate 36g (Dietary Fiber 1g); Protein 6g **Exchanges:** 2 Starch, ½ Other Carbohydrate, ½ Fat **Carbohydrate Choices:** 2½

Swedish Limpa Rye Bread

2 loaves (12 slices each) • Prep Time: 20 Minutes • Start to Finish: 3 Hours 35 Minutes

1½ cups warm water (120°F to 130°F)

2 envelopes (2¼ teaspoons each) active dry yeast

¼ cup molasses

⅓ cup sugar

1 teaspoon salt

2 tablespoons butter, softened

2 teaspoons grated orange peel (1 large orange)

2½ cups rye flour

2¼ to 2¾ cups all-purpose flour

Cornmeal

1 Pour warm water into large bowl and sprinkle yeast on top. Stir until dissolved. Stir in molasses, sugar, salt, butter, orange peel and rye flour. Beat with wooden spoon until smooth. Stir in 2 cups of the all-purpose flour. Stir in enough remaining all-purpose flour until dough pulls away from sides of bowl.

2 Place dough on lightly floured surface; cover with bowl. Let rest 15 minutes. Knead 5 minutes or until smooth and elastic. Spray large bowl with cooking spray. Place dough in bowl, turning to grease all sides. Cover with plastic wrap. Let rise in warm place 1 hour to 1 hour 30 minutes or until doubled in size. Gently punch dough down. Cover; let rise 40 minutes or until doubled in size.

3 Spray cookie sheet with cooking spray; sprinkle with cornmeal. Punch dough down to remove bubbles; divide dough in half. Shape each half into round loaf; flatten slightly. Place loaves on cookie sheet, 2 inches apart. Cover; let rise 1 hour. Heat oven to 375°F.

4 Uncover loaves. Bake 30 to 35 minutes or until golden brown.

1 Slice: Calories 110; Total Fat 1.5g (Saturated Fat 0.5g, Trans Fat 0g); Cholesterol 0mg; Sodium 110mg; Total Carbohydrate 23g (Dietary Fiber 2g); Protein 2g **Exchanges:** 1 Starch, ½ Other Carbohydrate **Carbohydrate Choices:** 1½

Fluffy Spoon Bread

10 servings (½ cup each) • Prep Time: 15 Minutes • Start to Finish: 1 Hour

1½ cups boiling water
1 cup yellow cornmeal
1 tablespoon butter, softened
3 eggs, separated
1 cup buttermilk
1 teaspoon salt
1 teaspoon sugar
1 teaspoon baking powder
¼ teaspoon baking soda

1 Heat oven to 375°F. Grease 2-quart casserole. In large bowl, stir together boiling water and cornmeal until well blended. Beat in butter and egg yolks with wire whisk or fork until well blended. Stir in remaining ingredients except egg whites.

2 In medium bowl, beat egg whites just until soft peaks form; fold into cornmeal mixture. Pour batter into casserole.

3 Bake 45 to 50 minutes or until set and deep golden brown.

1 Serving: Calories 110; Total Fat 3.5g (Saturated Fat 1.5g, Trans Fat 0g); Cholesterol 60mg; Sodium 370mg; Total Carbohydrate 14g (Dietary Fiber 0g); Protein 4g **Exchanges:** 1 Starch, ½ Fat **Carbohydrate Choices:** 1

Irish Soda Bread

1 loaf (14 slices) • Prep Time: 10 Minutes • Start to Finish: 55 Minutes

2½   cups all-purpose flour

2   tablespoons sugar

1   teaspoon baking soda

1   teaspoon baking powder

½   teaspoon salt

3   tablespoons butter, softened

⅓   cup raisins, if desired

¾   cup buttermilk

1   Heat oven to 375°F. Grease cookie sheet. In large bowl, mix flour, sugar, baking soda, baking powder and salt. Using pastry blender or fork, cut in butter until mixture resembles fine crumbs. Stir in raisins and just enough buttermilk so dough leaves sides of bowl.

2   Turn dough onto lightly floured surface. Knead 1 to 2 minutes or until smooth. Shape into round loaf, about 6½ inches in diameter. Place on cookie sheet. Cut an X shape about ½ inch deep through loaf with floured knife.

3   Bake 35 to 45 minutes or until golden brown. Brush with softened butter, if desired.

1 Slice: Calories 120; Total Fat 3g (Saturated Fat 2g, Trans Fat 0g); Cholesterol 10mg; Sodium 240mg; Total Carbohydrate 20g (Dietary Fiber 0g); Protein 3g **Exchanges:** 1 Starch, ½ Other Carbohydrate, ½ Fat **Carbohydrate Choices:** 1

Pumpkin-Cranberry Pecan Bread with Boozy Whipped Cream

1 loaf (12 slices) • Prep Time: 15 Minutes • Start to Finish: 3 Hours 10 Minutes

BREAD

- ½ cup butter, melted
- ½ cup granulated sugar
- ¼ cup packed light brown sugar
- 2 eggs
- 1¼ cups canned pumpkin (not pumpkin pie mix)
- ¾ cup milk
- 2½ cups all-purpose flour
- 1 teaspoon baking powder
- ¾ teaspoon baking soda
- ½ teaspoon salt
- ½ teaspoon ground cinnamon
- ½ teaspoon ground allspice
- ½ teaspoon ground nutmeg
- ½ teaspoon ground ginger
- 1 cup chopped pecans, toasted*
- ½ cup sweetened dried cranberries

TOPPING, IF DESIRED

- 1 cup heavy whipping cream
- 1 tablespoon Grand Marnier or orange juice
- 1 tablespoon powdered sugar

1 Heat oven to 325°F. Spray 9x5-inch loaf pan with baking spray with flour.

2 In large bowl, beat butter, granulated sugar and brown sugar with electric mixer on low speed until smooth. Mix in eggs, pumpkin and milk. Stir in flour, baking powder, baking soda, salt and spices until blended. Stir in pecans and cranberries. Spoon batter into pan.

3 Bake 1 hour 5 minutes to 1 hour 15 minutes or until toothpick inserted into center comes out clean (crack on top surface should look dry). Cool 10 minutes; remove from pan to cooling rack. Cool completely, about 1 hour 30 minutes.

4 In chilled large, deep bowl, beat topping ingredients with electric mixer on low speed until mixture begins to thicken. Gradually increase speed to high and beat until stiff peaks form. Slice bread; serve with a dollop of topping.

* To toast pecans, heat oven to 325°F. Spread pecans in ungreased shallow pan. Bake uncovered 8 to 10 minutes, stirring occasionally, until light brown.

1 Slice: Calories 330; Total Fat 16g (Saturated Fat 6g, Trans Fat 0g); Cholesterol 55mg; Sodium 380mg; Total Carbohydrate 41g (Dietary Fiber 3g); Protein 5g **Exchanges:** 1 Starch, 1½ Other Carbohydrate, ½ High-Fat Meat, 2½ Fat **Carbohydrate Choices:** 3

CHAPTER FOUR

Salads & Sides

As the story goes, this recipe was created at the Waldorf Astoria hotel in New York City. It's great as a side salad, or mix it up and use it as a surprising sandwich filling.

WALDORF SALAD

4 servings (¾ cup each) • Prep Time: 10 Minutes • Start to Finish: 10 Minutes

½ cup mayonnaise or salad dressing

1 tablespoon lemon juice

1 tablespoon milk

2 medium unpeeled red apples, coarsely chopped (2 cups)

2 medium stalks celery, chopped (1 cup)

⅓ cup coarsely chopped nuts

Salad greens, if desired

1 In medium bowl, mix mayonnaise, lemon juice and milk until blended.

2 Stir in apples, celery and nuts. Serve on salad greens. Store salad covered in refrigerator.

1 Serving: Calories 310; Total Fat 27g (Saturated Fat 4g, Trans Fat 0g); Cholesterol 10mg; Sodium 190mg; Total Carbohydrate 15g (Dietary Fiber 3g); Protein 2g **Exchanges:** 1 Starch, 5½ Fat **Carbohydrate Choices:** 1

BLAST FROM THE PAST:

(*Betty Crocker Picture Cook Book,* 1950)
At the White House, Washington, DC

President and Mrs. Dwight D. Eisenhower mention this 1956 dinner menu as one of their favorites, and it is one that almost any American citizen can enjoy in his or her own home.

Broiled Sirloin Steak

Baked Potatoes

Green Beans

Green Salad with French Dressing

Apple Pie with Cheese

Coffee

Apple-Grapefruit Salad

6 servings • Prep Time: 20 Minutes • Start to Finish: 20 Minutes

LIME-HONEY DRESSING

- 3 tablespoons frozen (thawed) limeade or lemonade concentrate
- 3 tablespoons honey
- 3 tablespoons vegetable oil or sour cream
- ¼ teaspoon poppy seed

SALAD

- Salad greens
- 3 unpeeled red or green apples, sliced
- 2 grapefruits, peeled, sectioned
- ½ cup pomegranate seeds

1 In tightly covered container, shake all dressing ingredients until well blended. Refrigerate until serving time.

2 Arrange salad greens on individual salad plates; top with apple slices, grapefruit sections and pomegranate seeds. Serve with dressing.

1 Serving: Calories 190; Total Fat 7g (Saturated Fat 1g, Trans Fat 0g); Cholesterol 0mg; Sodium 0mg; Total Carbohydrate 33g (Dietary Fiber 3g); Protein 1g **Exchanges:** 2 Fruit, 1½ Fat **Carbohydrate Choices:** 2½

BETTY'S KITCHEN TIP

Yes, it takes a few extra minutes to extract the bright red seeds from a pomegranate, but their sparkling sweet-tart flavor makes it all worthwhile. To get at the seeds, cut a pomegranate in half and dig the seeds out with a spoon, removing any light-colored membrane that may adhere. Or you can purchase just the seeds.

Seven-Layer Salad

6 servings (about 1¼ cups each) • Prep Time: 25 Minutes • Start to Finish: 2 Hours 25 Minutes

1 package (9 oz) frozen green peas

6 cups bite-size pieces mixed salad greens

2 medium stalks celery, thinly sliced (1 cup)

1 cup thinly sliced radishes

8 medium green onions, sliced (½ cup)

4 slices bacon, crisply cooked and crumbled

½ cup mayonnaise or salad dressing

1 cup plain yogurt

¼ cup grated Parmesan cheese or shredded Cheddar cheese (1 oz)

1 Cook peas as directed on package; rinse with cold water and drain.

2 Place salad greens in large glass bowl. Layer celery, radishes, green onions, bacon and peas on salad greens.

3 Mix mayonnaise and yogurt in small bowl; spread over peas, covering top completely and sealing to edge of bowl. Sprinkle with cheese.

4 Cover and refrigerate at least 2 hours to blend flavors but no longer than 12 hours. Toss before serving if desired. Store covered in refrigerator.

1 Serving: Calories 250; Total Fat 18g (Saturated Fat 4g, Trans Fat 0g); Cholesterol 20mg; Sodium 340mg; Total Carbohydrate 14g (Dietary Fiber 4g); Protein 9g **Exchanges:** ½ Starch, 1 Vegetable, ½ Medium-Fat Meat, 3 Fat **Carbohydrate Choices:** 1

Comfort food never goes out of style!

Mandarin Salad with Sugared Almonds

6 servings (1⅓ cups each) • Prep Time: 30 Minutes • Start to Finish: 30 Minutes

SUGARED ALMONDS

- ¼ cup sliced almonds
- 4 teaspoons sugar

SWEET-SOUR DRESSING

- ¼ cup vegetable oil
- 2 tablespoons sugar
- 2 tablespoons white or cider vinegar
- 1 tablespoon chopped fresh parsley
- ½ teaspoon salt

  Dash pepper

  Dash red pepper sauce

SALAD

- 3 cups bite-size pieces mixed salad greens or iceberg lettuce
- 3 cups bite-size pieces romaine lettuce
- 2 medium stalks celery, chopped (1 cup)
- 2 medium green onions, thinly sliced (2 tablespoons)
- 1 can (11 oz) mandarin orange segments, drained

1 In 1-quart saucepan, cook almonds and 4 teaspoons sugar over low heat about 10 minutes, stirring constantly, until sugar is melted and almonds are coated. Cool; break apart.

2 Meanwhile, in tightly covered container, shake dressing ingredients. Refrigerate until serving time.

3 In large bowl, mix salad ingredients. Shake dressing; pour over salad and toss until coated. Sprinkle with sugared almonds. Serve immediately.

1 Serving: Calories 170; Total Fat 12g (Saturated Fat 1.5g, Trans Fat 0g); Cholesterol 0mg; Sodium 220mg; Total Carbohydrate 15g (Dietary Fiber 2g); Protein 2g **Exchanges:** ½ Fruit, 2 Vegetable, 2 Fat **Carbohydrate Choices:** 1

EASY CRANBERRY-ORANGE MOLD

8 servings • Prep Time: 10 Minutes • Start to Finish: 4 Hours 10 Minutes

1   can (11 oz) mandarin orange segments, drained, juice reserved

1   box (4-serving size) orange-flavored gelatin

1   can (14 oz) whole berry cranberry sauce

Salad greens, if desired

1   Spray 4-cup mold with cooking spray. Add enough water to reserved mandarin orange juice to measure 1¼ cups. In 1-quart saucepan, heat juice mixture to boiling.

2   In medium bowl, pour boiling mixture on gelatin; stir until gelatin is dissolved. Stir in cranberry sauce until sauce is melted. Stir in orange segments. Pour into mold.

3   Refrigerate about 4 hours or until firm. Unmold; serve on salad greens.

1 Serving: Calories 150; Total Fat 0g (Saturated Fat 0g, Trans Fat 0g); Cholesterol 0mg; Sodium 65mg; Total Carbohydrate 35g (Dietary Fiber 1g, Sugars 33g); Protein 1g **Exchanges:** 2½ Fruit **Carbohydrate Choices:** 2

CRANBERRY STREUSEL SWEET POTATOES

8 servings • Prep Time: 15 Minutes • Start to Finish: 1 Hour 15 Minutes

6 medium dark-orange sweet potatoes (2 lb), peeled and cut into small pieces

2 tablespoons butter

½ teaspoon salt

½ cup soft bread crumbs (about 1 slice bread)

¼ cup dried cranberries

¼ cup coarsely chopped pecans

2 tablespoons butter, melted

1 Place sweet potatoes in 3-quart saucepan; add enough water just to cover potatoes. Cover pan and heat to boiling; reduce heat. Simmer covered 10 to 15 minutes or until potatoes are tender when pierced with a fork; drain. Return potatoes to saucepan. Shake pan with potatoes over low heat to dry (this will help mashed potatoes be fluffier).

2 Heat oven to 350°F. Mash potatoes, 2 tablespoons butter and salt in medium bowl with potato masher or electric mixer on low speed until no lumps remain. Spoon into ungreased 1-quart casserole. Mix remaining ingredients; sprinkle over potatoes.

3 Bake uncovered about 30 minutes or until potatoes are hot and topping mixture is golden brown.

1 Serving: Calories 200; Total Fat 9g (Saturated Fat 4g, Trans Fat 0g); Cholesterol 15mg; Sodium 300mg; Total Carbohydrate 28g (Dietary Fiber 4g); Protein 2g **Exchanges:** 1 Starch, 1 Other Carbohydrate, 1½ Fat **Carbohydrate Choices:** 2

BETTY'S DO-AHEAD TIP

You can make these super potatoes a day ahead. Just follow the directions through Step 2, then cover and refrigerate up to 24 hours. Bake uncovered 45 to 60 minutes or until potatoes are hot and topping mixture is golden brown.

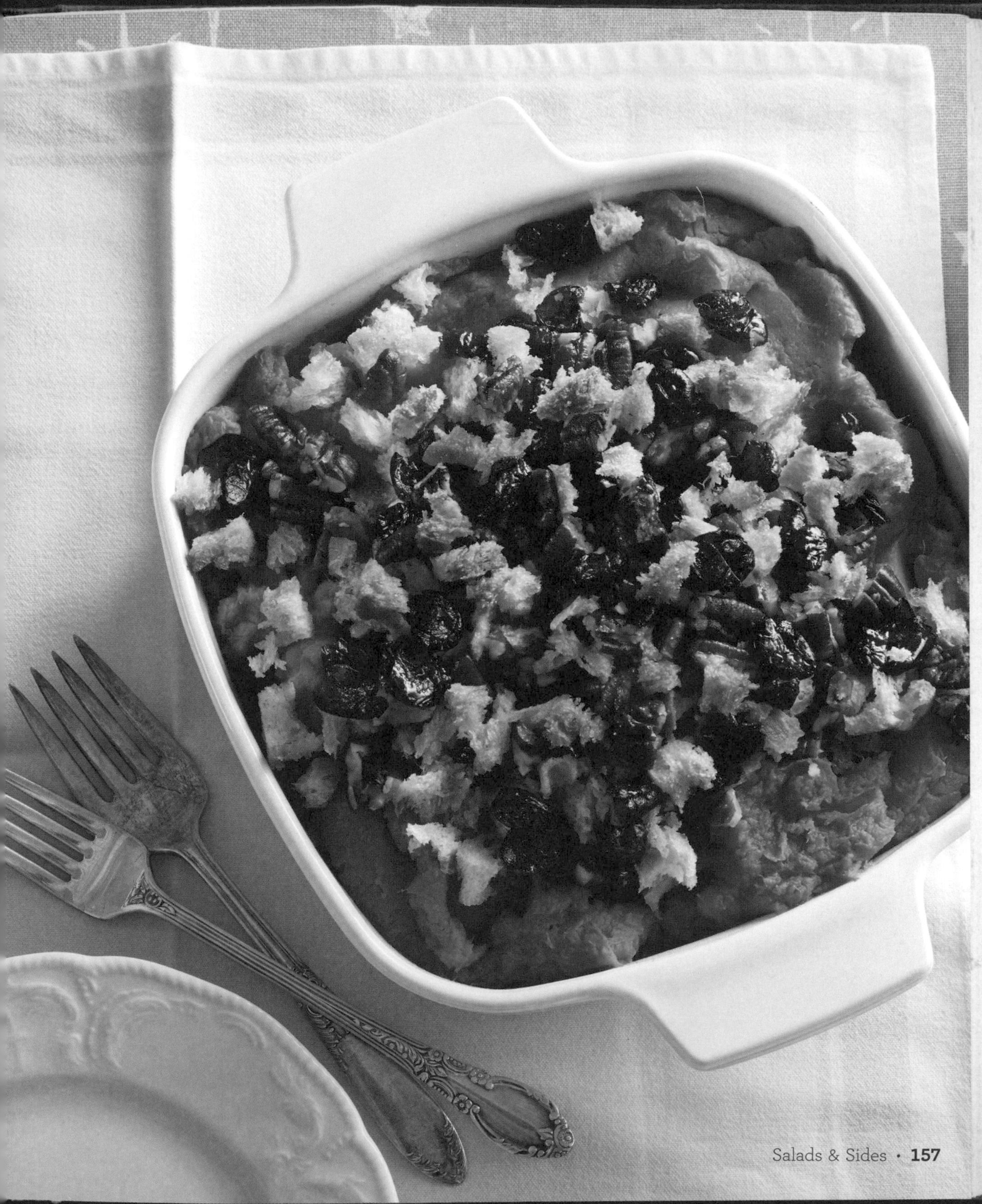

Healthified Lemon-Broccoli Salad

8 servings (½ cup each) • Prep Time: 20 Minutes • Start to Finish: 1 Hour 20 Minutes

3 tablespoons light mayonnaise or salad dressing

2 tablespoons plain Greek yogurt

¼ teaspoon finely grated lemon peel

2 teaspoons lemon juice

¼ teaspoon peeled, grated fresh ginger

4 cups small broccoli and/or cauliflower florets

⅓ cup finely chopped red onion

¼ cup dried cranberries

3 tablespoons roasted soy nuts

1 In a large bowl, stir together mayonnaise, yogurt, lemon peel, lemon juice and ginger. Add broccoli, red onion, and cranberries. Toss to coat. Cover and chill for 1 to 24 hours.

2 Just before serving, sprinkle with soy nuts.

1 Serving: Calories 60; Total Fat 2.5g (Saturated Fat 0.5g, Trans Fat 0g); Cholesterol 0mg; Sodium 55mg; Total Carbohydrate 8g (Dietary Fiber 2g); Protein 3g **Exchanges:** ½ Other Carbohydrate, ½ Vegetable, ½ Fat **Carbohydrate Choices:** ½

BLAST FROM THE PAST:

(*Betty Crocker Picture Cook Book*, 1950)
A Mother Can Give Her Family a Priceless Gift

Why are some mothers tired all the time and some children fighting colds all winter? Probably because they don't eat the right things. Food that abundantly nourishes can make the difference between a family that just lives and one that has enough and more of health and vigor. You probably know this if you and your family are eating the right foods: all of you have the extra vitality to meet health hazards and the extra enthusiasm to welcome challenges and opportunities.

Hot German Potato Salad

6 servings (⅔ cup each) • Prep Time: 10 Minutes • Start to Finish: 1 Hour 5 Minutes

4   medium red or white potatoes, unpeeled (1½ lb)

3   slices bacon, cut into 1-inch pieces

1   medium onion, chopped (½ cup)

1   tablespoon all-purpose flour

1   tablespoon sugar

½   teaspoon salt

¼   teaspoon celery seed

    Dash pepper

½   cup water

¼   cup white or cider vinegar

1 In 3-quart saucepan, place potatoes and just enough water to cover potatoes. Cover pan and heat to boiling; reduce heat to low. Cook 30 to 35 minutes or until tender; drain. Let stand until cool enough to handle. Cut potatoes into ¼-inch slices.

2 In 10-inch skillet, cook bacon over medium heat 8 to 10 minutes, stirring occasionally, until crisp. Remove bacon with slotted spoon; drain on paper towels.

3 Cook onion in bacon drippings in skillet over medium heat, stirring occasionally, until tender. Stir in flour, sugar, salt, celery seed and pepper. Cook over low heat, stirring constantly, until mixture is bubbly; remove from heat.

4 Stir in water and vinegar. Heat to boiling, stirring constantly. Boil and stir 1 minute; remove from heat. Stir in potatoes and bacon. Heat over medium heat, stirring gently to coat potato slices, until hot and bubbly. Serve warm.

1 Serving: Calories 120; Total Fat 2g (Saturated Fat 0.5g, Trans Fat 0g); Cholesterol 0mg; Sodium 270mg; Total Carbohydrate 22g (Dietary Fiber 3g); Protein 3g **Exchanges:** 1 Starch, 1 Vegetable, ½ Fat **Carbohydrate Choices:** 1½

Nutty Baked Squash

4 servings • Prep Time: 15 Minutes • Start to Finish: 45 Minutes

2 acorn squash (1 lb each)

⅔ cup round buttery cracker crumbs (20 crackers)

⅓ cup coarsely chopped pecans

3 tablespoons packed brown sugar

½ teaspoon salt

¼ teaspoon ground nutmeg

⅓ cup butter, melted

1 Heat oven to 400°F. Cut each squash in half. Remove seeds and fibers. In medium bowl, mix remaining ingredients until blended. Spoon evenly into squash halves. Place filled squash halves in 13x9-inch pan; cover tightly with foil.

2 Bake 30 minutes. Uncover; bake 10 to 15 minutes longer or until squash is fork-tender.

1 Serving: Calories 420; Total Fat 26g (Saturated Fat 11g, Trans Fat 0.5g); Cholesterol 40mg; Sodium 520mg; Total Carbohydrate 43g (Dietary Fiber 8g); Protein 3g **Exchanges:** 1 Starch, 2 Other Carbohydrate, 5 Fat **Carbohydrate Choices:** 3

WILD RICE WITH MUSHROOMS AND ALMONDS

6 servings • Prep Time: 30 Minutes • Start to Finish: 2 Hours

1 cup uncooked wild rice

¼ cup butter

½ cup slivered almonds

2 tablespoons chopped green onions

8 oz sliced fresh mushrooms

3 cups chicken broth

1 Heat oven to 325°F. Rinse wild rice; drain well.

2 In 10-inch skillet, melt butter over medium heat. Stir in rice, almonds, green onions and mushrooms. Cook 10 to 15 minutes or until almonds are golden and rice is toasted, stirring occasionally. Spoon rice mixture into ungreased 3-quart casserole. Add broth; stir well. Cover tightly.

3 Bake 1 hour 30 minutes or until liquid is absorbed and rice is tender.

1 Serving: Calories 250; Total Fat 13g (Saturated Fat 5g, Trans Fat 0g); Cholesterol 25mg; Sodium 530mg; Total Carbohydrate 26g (Dietary Fiber 3g); Protein 8g **Exchanges:** 1 Starch, ½ Other Carbohydrate, 1 Vegetable, ½ High-Fat Meat, 1½ Fat **Carbohydrate Choices:** 2

Cauliflower and Carrot Gratin

....

14 servings (½ cup each) • Prep Time: 25 Minutes • Start to Finish: 1 Hour

....

1 bag (16 oz) ready-to-eat baby-cut carrots

1 head (about 2½ lb) fresh cauliflower, cut into florets (6 cups)

6 tablespoons butter

1 medium onion, finely chopped (½ cup)

3 tablespoons all-purpose flour

1 teaspoon salt

1 teaspoon ground mustard

1½ cups milk

6 oz (about 8 slices) American cheese, cut into small pieces

½ cup panko bread crumbs

1 Heat oven to 350°F. Spray 2½-quart casserole with cooking spray.

2 In 5-quart Dutch oven, heat 8 cups water to boiling. Add carrots; boil uncovered 10 minutes. Add cauliflower; boil 4 minutes longer. Drain; set aside.

3 Meanwhile, in 4-quart saucepan, melt 3 tablespoons of the butter. Cook onion in butter about 4 minutes, stirring occasionally, until softened. Stir in flour, salt and mustard with whisk; cook about 1 minute or until bubbly. Slowly stir in milk. Cook and stir until bubbly and slightly thickened. Remove from heat; stir in cheese until melted. Stir in carrots and cauliflower. Pour into casserole.

4 In small microwavable bowl, microwave remaining 3 tablespoons butter on High 1 minute or until melted; stir in bread crumbs. Sprinkle over vegetable mixture.

5 Bake uncovered 25 to 30 minutes or until bubbly around edges. Let stand 5 minutes before serving.

1 Serving: Calories 160; Total Fat 10g (Saturated Fat 6g, Trans Fat 0g); Cholesterol 30mg; Sodium 330mg; Total Carbohydrate 11g (Dietary Fiber 2g); Protein 5g **Exchanges:** ½ Starch, 1 Vegetable, 2 Fat **Carbohydrate Choices:** 1

BETTY'S KITCHEN TIPS

Look in the frozen-food case for bags of frozen chopped onions. Keep them on hand for fuss-free chopped onion.

American cheese can be purchased in bulk at most supermarket delis. Simply ask them to cut off the size chunk you desire, and either chop or shred it before adding to the milk mixture.

To cut down on last-minute details before a dinner party, have the cauliflower washed and cut into florets, chop the onion and have the cheese cut into pieces. You can even mix the bread crumbs and butter together and store covered in a small bowl.

BLAST FROM THE PAST:

(Betty Crocker Picture Cook Book, 1950)
Original "All You Have to Do" Tip

To make cooked carrots particularly appealing: serve whole, buttered, or glazed carrots with a sprig of green parsley pushed in the end (to look like fresh carrots).

Chicken-Thyme Penne

8 servings • Prep Time: 25 Minutes • Start to Finish: 4 Hours 25 Minutes

3 cups uncooked penne pasta (9 oz)

4 cups cubed cooked chicken

2 cups seedless red grapes, halved

2 medium stalks celery, sliced (1 cup)

⅓ cup chopped onion

3 tablespoons olive or vegetable oil

2 tablespoons chopped fresh or 2 teaspoons dried thyme, crushed

1¼ cups mayonnaise or salad dressing

1 tablespoon milk

1 tablespoon honey

1 tablespoon coarse-grained mustard

1 teaspoon salt

1 cup chopped walnuts, toasted*

1. In 4-quart saucepan, cook pasta as directed on package. Rinse with cold water; drain.

2. In very large (4-quart) bowl, mix pasta, chicken, grapes, celery and onion. In small bowl, mix oil and 1 tablespoon of the fresh thyme (or 1 teaspoon of the dried thyme). Pour over chicken mixture; toss to coat.

3. In small bowl, mix mayonnaise, milk, honey, mustard, salt and remaining 1 tablespoon fresh thyme (or 1 teaspoon dried thyme). Cover chicken mixture and mayonnaise mixture separately; refrigerate at least 4 hours but no longer than 24 hours.

4. Up to 2 hours before serving, toss chicken mixture and mayonnaise mixture. Cover; refrigerate. Just before serving, stir in ¾ cup of the walnuts. Sprinkle salad with remaining ¼ cup walnuts.

*To toast walnuts, sprinkle in ungreased skillet. Cook over medium heat 5 to 7 minutes, stirring frequently until walnuts begin to brown, then stirring constantly until nuts are light brown.

1 Serving: Calories 690; Total Fat 46g (Saturated Fat 7g, Trans Fat 0g); Cholesterol 80mg; Sodium 600mg; Total Carbohydrate 41g (Dietary Fiber 4g); Protein 29g **Exchanges:** 2 Starch, 1 Fruit, 3 Medium-Fat Meat, 5½ Fat **Carbohydrate Choices:** 3

TUNA-MACARONI SALAD

6 servings (1 cup each) • Prep Time: 20 Minutes • Start to Finish: 1 Hour 20 Minutes

1 package (7 oz) elbow macaroni

½ cup frozen green peas, thawed

1 can (9 oz) tuna, drained

1 cup mayonnaise or salad dressing

1 cup shredded Cheddar cheese (4 oz), if desired

¼ cup sweet pickle relish, if desired

2 teaspoons lemon juice

¾ teaspoon salt

¼ teaspoon pepper

1 medium stalk celery, chopped (½ cup)

1 small onion, chopped (¼ cup)

1 Cook macaroni as directed on package, adding peas for last 4 to 6 minutes of cooking; rinse with cold water and drain.

2 In large bowl, mix macaroni, peas and remaining ingredients. Cover and refrigerate at least 1 hour to blend flavors.

1 Serving: Calories 450; Total Fat 30g (Saturated Fat 4.5g, Trans Fat 0g); Cholesterol 35mg; Sodium 780mg; Total Carbohydrate 29g (Dietary Fiber 3g); Protein 15g **Exchanges:** 2 Starch, 1½ Very Lean Meat, 5½ Fat **Carbohydrate Choices:** 2

MANGO PORK FRIED RICE

8 servings • Prep Time: 25 Minutes • Start to Finish: 25 Minutes

1 tablespoon vegetable oil

1 cup sliced fresh mushrooms (3 oz)

1 tablespoon peeled, finely chopped fresh ginger

1 clove garlic, finely chopped

¾ cup diced cooked pork

1 can (8 oz) sliced water chestnuts, drained

6 medium green onions, sliced (about ⅓ cup)

3 cups cold cooked rice

1 cup frozen green peas, thawed

2 teaspoons reduced-sodium soy sauce

Dash pepper

1 large mango, seed removed, peeled and diced (1½ cups)

1 In 12-inch nonstick skillet, heat 1½ teaspoons of the oil over medium-high heat until hot. Add mushrooms, ginger and garlic. Cook and stir 2 to 3 minutes or until mushrooms are tender. Add pork, water chestnuts and green onions; heat through. Remove from skillet; cover and keep warm.

2 Heat remaining 1½ teaspoons oil in same skillet over medium-high heat. Add rice and peas to skillet. Cook and stir 3 minutes. Stir in soy sauce and pepper. Add pork mixture and mango. Cook and stir 2 minutes or until heated through.

1 Serving: Calories 170; Total Fat 3g (Saturated Fat 0.5g, Trans Fat 0g); Cholesterol 10mg; Sodium 290mg; Total Carbohydrate 30g (Dietary Fiber 2g); Protein 7g **Exchanges:** 1½ Starch, ½ Fruit, ½ Vegetable, ½ Lean Meat **Carbohydrate Choices:** 2

THREE-BEAN CASSEROLE

8 servings (1⅓ cups each) • Prep Time: 10 Minutes • Start to Finish: 1 Hour 5 Minutes

1 lb lean (at least 80%) ground beef

2 medium stalks celery, sliced (1 cup)

1 medium onion, chopped (½ cup)

1 large clove garlic, finely chopped

2 cans (16 oz each) baked beans (any variety), undrained

1 can (15 to 16 oz) lima or butter beans, drained, rinsed

1 can (15 to 15.5 oz) kidney beans, drained, rinsed

1 cup barbecue sauce

1 tablespoon ground mustard

2 tablespoons honey or packed brown sugar

1 tablespoon white or cider vinegar

¼ teaspoon red pepper sauce

1 Heat oven to 400°F. In 10-inch skillet, cook beef, celery, onion and garlic over medium heat 8 to 10 minutes, stirring occasionally, until beef is no longer pink; drain.

2 In ungreased 3-quart casserole, mix beef mixture and remaining ingredients. Bake uncovered about 45 minutes, stirring once, until hot and bubbly.

1 Serving: Calories 420; Total Fat 10g (Saturated Fat 3g, Trans Fat 0g); Cholesterol 20mg; Sodium 1400mg; Total Carbohydrate 62g (Dietary Fiber 16g); Protein 22g **Exchanges:** 4 Starch, 1 Fat **Carbohydrate Choices:** 4

Creamy corn bakes into old-fashioned comfort food. This cheesy version is a mainstay for many family gatherings.

Classic Baked Corn Pudding

16 servings (½ cup each) • Prep Time: 20 Minutes • Start to Finish: 1 Hour 35 Minutes

½ cup butter

1 small onion, chopped (¼ cup)

½ cup all-purpose flour

½ teaspoon salt

½ teaspoon pepper

4 cups milk (1 quart)

6 eggs, slightly beaten

2 cups shredded Cheddar cheese (8 oz)

2 bags (12 oz each) frozen whole kernel corn, thawed, drained

½ cup chopped fresh parsley or 2 tablespoons parsley flakes

¾ cup plain dry bread crumbs

3 tablespoons butter, melted

1 Heat oven to 350°F. Spray 13x9-inch (3-quart) glass baking dish or 3-quart casserole with cooking spray.

2 In 4-quart Dutch oven or saucepan, melt ½ cup butter over medium heat. Add onion; cook 3 to 4 minutes, stirring frequently, until tender. Stir in flour, salt and pepper until well blended. Stir in milk. Cook 4 to 5 minutes, stirring constantly, until thickened. Gradually stir in eggs and cheese. Stir in corn and parsley. Pour into baking dish.

3 In small bowl, mix bread crumbs and 3 tablespoons melted butter; sprinkle over corn mixture.

4 Bake uncovered 55 to 65 minutes or until mixture is set and knife inserted in center comes out clean. Let stand 5 to 10 minutes before serving.

1 Serving: Calories 260; Total Fat 16g (Saturated Fat 10g, Trans Fat 0g); Cholesterol 120mg; Sodium 310mg; Total Carbohydrate 18g (Dietary Fiber 1g); Protein 10g **Exchanges:** 1 Starch, 1 High-Fat Meat, 1½ Fat **Carbohydrate Choices:** 1

Desserts

Caramel Snickerdoodle Cake

16 servings • Prep Time: 20 Minutes • Start to Finish: 2 Hours 40 Minutes

1¾ cups plus 2 tablespoons sugar

2 teaspoons ground cinnamon

2½ cups all-purpose flour

2 teaspoons baking soda

1 teaspoon salt

1 can (5 oz) evaporated milk

1 cup sour cream

½ cup butter or margarine, melted

1 teaspoon vanilla

2 eggs, beaten

10 caramels, unwrapped

1 Heat oven to 350°F. Grease 12-cup fluted tube cake pan with shortening. In small bowl, mix 2 tablespoons of the sugar and 1 teaspoon of the cinnamon. Sprinkle mixture over inside of pan, turning to evenly coat. Shake out any excess.

2 In large bowl, mix remaining 1¾ cups sugar, remaining 1 teaspoon cinnamon, the flour, baking soda and salt. Reserve 1 tablespoon of the evaporated milk for the topping. Stir remaining evaporated milk, sour cream, melted butter, vanilla and eggs into dry ingredients until well blended. Pour batter into pan.

3 Bake 40 to 50 minutes or until toothpick inserted in center comes out clean. Let stand 30 minutes; remove from pan. Cool completely, about 1 hour.

4 In small microwavable bowl, melt caramels with reserved evaporated milk uncovered on High 1 to 2 minutes, stirring every 30 seconds, until caramels are melted and mixture is smooth. Drizzle over cooled cake.

1 Serving: Calories 340; Total Fat 11g (Saturated Fat 6g, Trans Fat 0g); Cholesterol 50mg; Sodium 420mg; Total Carbohydrate 54g (Dietary Fiber 0g); Protein 4g **Exchanges:** 1½ Starch, 2 Other Carbohydrate, 2 Fat
Carbohydrate Choices: 3½

Starlight Yellow Cake

12 servings • Prep Time: 20 Minutes • Start to Finish: 2 Hours 10 Minutes

2¼ cups all-purpose flour

1½ cups sugar

3½ teaspoons baking powder

1 teaspoon salt

½ cup butter, softened

1¼ cups milk

1 teaspoon vanilla

3 eggs

Chocolate Frosting (below), if desired

CHOCOLATE FROSTING

⅓ cup butter, softened

3 oz unsweetened baking chocolate, melted, cooled 5 minutes

3 cups powdered sugar

2 teaspoons vanilla

3 to 4 tablespoons milk

1 Heat oven to 350°F. Grease bottoms and sides of 2 (9-inch) round cake pans, 3 (8-inch) round cake pans or 1 (13x9-inch) rectangular pan with shortening; lightly flour and tap out excess.

2 In large bowl, beat all ingredients except frosting with electric mixer on low speed 30 seconds, scraping bowl constantly. Beat on high speed 3 minutes, scraping bowl occasionally. Pour batter into pan(s).

3 Bake 9-inch pans 25 to 30 minutes, 8-inch pans 30 to 35 minutes or 13x9-inch pan 35 to 40 minutes, or until toothpick inserted in center comes out clean or cake springs back when touched lightly in center. Cool rounds 10 minutes; remove from pans to cooling racks. Cool 13x9-inch cake in pan on cooling rack. Cool completely, about 1 hour.

4 In large bowl, beat ⅓ cup butter and chocolate with electric mixer on low speed until blended. Gradually beat in powdered sugar until blended. Gradually beat in 2 teaspoons vanilla and just enough of the 3 to 4 tablespoons milk to make frosting smooth and spreadable. If frosting is too thick, beat in more milk, a few drops at a time. If frosting becomes too thin, beat in a smallamount of powdered sugar.

5 Fill and frost round layers or frost top of 13x9-inch cake with frosting.

1 Serving: Calories 290; Total Fat 10g (Saturated Fat 4.5g, Trans Fat 0g); Cholesterol 75mg; Sodium 420mg; Total Carbohydrate 45g (Dietary Fiber 0g); Protein 5g
Exchanges: 2 Starch, 1 Other Carbohydrate, 1½ Fat **Carbohydrate Choices:** 3

VELVET CRUMB CAKE

8 servings • Prep Time: 20 Minutes • Start to Finish: 1 Hour

CAKE

1½ cups Original Bisquick mix

½ cup granulated sugar

½ cup milk or water

2 tablespoons shortening

1 teaspoon vanilla

1 egg

TOPPING

½ cup flaked coconut

⅓ cup packed brown sugar

¼ cup chopped nuts

3 tablespoons butter, softened

2 tablespoons milk

1 Heat oven to 350°F. Grease 9-inch round cake pan or 8-inch square pan with shortening; lightly flour and tap out excess.

2 In large bowl, beat Bisquick mix, granulated sugar, ½ cup milk, shortening, vanilla and egg with electric mixer on low speed 30 seconds, scraping bowl constantly. Beat on medium speed 4 minutes, scraping bowl occasionally. Pour into pan.

3 Bake 30 to 35 minutes or until toothpick inserted in center comes out clean. Cool 5 minutes.

4 In small bowl, mix coconut, brown sugar, nuts, butter and 2 tablespoons milk. Spread topping over cake.

5 Set oven to broil. Broil cake with top about 3 inches from heat 2 to 3 minutes or until golden brown. Serve warm or cool completely.

1 Serving: Calories 320; Total Fat 16g (Saturated Fat 6g, Trans Fat 1.5g); Cholesterol 40mg; Sodium 340mg; Total Carbohydrate 40g (Dietary Fiber 0g); Protein 4g **Exchanges:** 1 Starch, 1½ Other Carbohydrate, 3 Fat **Carbohydrate Choices:** 2½

BLAST FROM THE PAST:

(*Betty Crocker Picture Cook Book*, 1956)
Formal Dessert Service

At a formal dinner, finger bowls are brought in on dessert plates (small lace doily under bowl), with dessert fork on plate at left of bowl and dessert spoon at right. Each guest places finger bowl and doily aside, above plate at left, and places fork at left and spoon at right of plate.

Gingerbread

9 servings • Prep Time: 10 Minutes • Start to Finish: 1 Hour 5 Minutes

GINGERBREAD

2⅓ cups all-purpose flour

1 teaspoon baking soda

1 teaspoon ground ginger

1 teaspoon ground cinnamon

½ teaspoon salt

½ cup butter, softened, or shortening

⅓ cup sugar

1 cup molasses*

¾ cup hot water

1 egg

SWEETENED WHIPPED CREAM

½ cup heavy whipping cream

1 tablespoon powdered or granulated sugar

½ teaspoon vanilla

1 Heat oven to 325°F. Grease bottom and sides of 9-inch square pan with shortening; lightly flour and tap out excess.

2 In large bowl, beat all gingerbread ingredients with electric mixer on low speed 30 seconds, scraping bowl constantly. Beat on medium speed 3 minutes, scraping bowl occasionally. Pour batter into pan.

3 Bake 50 to 55 minutes or until toothpick inserted in center comes out clean.

4 Chill bowl and beaters in freezer or refrigerate 10 to 20 minutes. In chilled medium, deep bowl, beat Sweetened Whipped Cream ingredients with electric mixer on low speed until mixture begins to thicken. Gradually increase speed to high and beat just until soft peaks form. Do not overbeat or mixture will curdle. Makes 1 cup. Serve with warm gingerbread.

*Full-flavor (dark) molasses will result in a bold and robust flavor. For milder flavor, use mild-flavor (light) molasses. For extra-mild molasses flavor, use ½ cup light molasses and ½ cup real maple syrup.

1 Serving: Calories 370; Total Fat 12g (Saturated Fat 3g, Trans Fat 2g); Cholesterol 25mg; Sodium 360mg; Total Carbohydrate 60g (Dietary Fiber 1g); Protein 4g **Exchanges:** 1 Starch, 3 Other Carbohydrate, 2 Fat **Carbohydrate Choices:** 4

BLAST FROM THE PAST:

About Gingerbread

Early American colonists made gingerbread much as we do today. When Lafayette returned to America in 1784, he went to Fredericksburg to visit George Washington's mother. She served him mint julep with "spiced gingerbread." Her recipe included "West India molasses," a "wine glass of brandy" and the "juice and rind of orange" in addition to the usual ingredients.

Also known as a Swiss Roll, these sponge cakes rolled up with a jelly filling date back to the mid- to late 1800s. Today, there have been many adaptations of both the cake and the fillings. Try one of our favorite versions below.

Jelly Roll

10 servings • Prep Time: 30 Minutes • Start to Finish: 1 Hour 15 Minutes

3   eggs
1   cup granulated sugar
⅓   cup water
1   teaspoon vanilla
¾   cup all-purpose flour
1   teaspoon baking powder
¼   teaspoon salt
    Powdered sugar
    About ⅔ cup jelly or jam

1   Heat oven to 375°F. Line 15x10x1-inch pan with waxed paper, foil or cooking parchment paper; generously grease paper or foil with shortening.

2   In medium bowl, beat eggs with electric mixer on high speed about 5 minutes or until very thick and lemon colored. Gradually beat in granulated sugar. Beat in water and vanilla on low speed. Gradually add flour, baking powder and salt, beating on low speed just until smooth. Pour batter into pan, spreading to corners.

3   Bake 12 to 15 minutes or until toothpick inserted in center comes out clean. Immediately loosen cake from sides of pan and turn upside down onto towel generously sprinkled with powdered sugar. Carefully remove paper. Trim off stiff edges of cake if necessary. While cake is hot, carefully roll cake and towel from narrow end. Cool on cooling rack at least 30 minutes.

4   Unroll cake and remove towel. Beat jelly slightly with fork to soften; spread over cake. Roll up cake again; place seam-side down on serving plate. Sprinkle with powdered sugar.

1 Serving: Calories 200; Total Fat 1.5g (Saturated Fat 0.5g, Trans Fat 0g); Cholesterol 65mg; Sodium 135mg; Total Carbohydrate 42g (Dietary Fiber 0g); Protein 3g **Exchanges:** 1 Starch, 2 Other Carbohydrate **Carbohydrate Choices:** 3

Chocolate Cake Roll Increase eggs to 4. Beat in ¼ cup unsweetened cocoa powder with the flour. If desired, fill cake with ice cream instead of jelly or jam. Spread 1 to 1½ pints (2 to 3 cups) slightly softened ice cream over cooled cake. Roll up cake; wrap in plastic wrap. Freeze about 4 hours or until firm.

Lemon Curd Jelly Roll Make cake as directed, adding 2 teaspoons grated lemon peel with the flour. Omit jelly; spread cake with ⅔ cup purchased lemon curd. Roll up as directed. Store covered in refrigerator.

Whipped Cream Jelly Roll Make cake as directed, except substitute ½ teaspoon almond extract for the vanilla. In small bowl, beat ½ cup whipping cream, 2 teaspoons powdered sugar and ¼ teaspoon almond extract with electric mixer until stiff peaks form. Spread over cake. Roll up as directed. Store covered in refrigerator.

Baked Alaska Cupcakes

24 cupcakes • Prep Time: 50 Minutes • Start to Finish: 3 Hours 45 Minutes

CUPCAKES

2¾	cups all-purpose flour
1	tablespoon baking powder
½	teaspoon salt
¾	cup shortening
1⅔	cups sugar
5	egg whites
2½	teaspoons vanilla
1¼	cups milk
1	quart strawberry ice cream, softened (4 cups)

MERINGUE

4	egg whites
¼	teaspoon cream of tartar
1½	teaspoons vanilla
⅔	cup sugar

1 Heat oven to 350°F. Place paper baking cup in each of 48 regular-size muffin cups; spray paper cups with baking spray with flour. In medium bowl, mix flour, baking powder and salt; set aside.

2 In large bowl, beat shortening with electric mixer on medium speed 30 seconds. Gradually add 1⅔ cups sugar, about ⅓ cup at a time, beating well after each addition and scraping bowl occasionally. Beat 2 minutes longer. Add 5 egg whites, one at a time, beating well after each addition. Beat in 2½ teaspoons vanilla. On low speed, alternately add flour mixture, about one-third at a time, and milk, about half at a time, beating just until blended.

3 Divide batter evenly among muffin cups, filling only one-third full.

4 Bake 10 to 14 minutes or until toothpick inserted in center comes out clean. Cool 5 minutes. Remove cupcakes from pans to cooling racks. Cool completely, about 15 minutes.

5 Place 24 cupcakes in freezer plastic bag and freeze for another use. On top of each of the remaining 24 cupcakes, spoon and spread 2 heaping tablespoons ice cream. Cover; freeze at least 2 hours or overnight, until ice cream is hardened.

6 Heat oven to 450°F. In medium bowl, beat 4 egg whites, cream of tartar and 1½ teaspoons vanilla with electric mixer on high speed until soft peaks form. Gradually add ⅔ cup sugar, 1 tablespoon at a time, beating until stiff peaks form and mixture is glossy. Spread over ice cream–topped cupcakes. Place on cookie sheet.

7 Bake 2 to 3 minutes or until lightly browned. Serve immediately.

1 Cupcake: Calories 250; Total Fat 9g (Saturated Fat 3.5g, Trans Fat 1g); Cholesterol 10mg; Sodium 150mg; Total Carbohydrate 36g (Dietary Fiber 0g); Protein 4g
Exchanges: 1½ Starch, 1 Other Carbohydrate, 1½ Fat
Carbohydrate Choices: 2½

Lemon Chiffon Cake

12 servings • Prep Time: 20 Minutes • Start to Finish: 3 Hours 35 Minutes

CAKE

- 2 cups all-purpose flour or 2¼ cups cake flour
- 1½ cups granulated sugar
- 1 tablespoon baking powder
- 1 teaspoon salt
- ¾ cup cold water
- ½ cup vegetable oil
- 2 teaspoons vanilla
- 1 tablespoon grated lemon peel
- 7 egg yolks (if using all-purpose flour) or 5 egg yolks (if using cake flour)
- 1 cup egg whites (about 8)
- ½ teaspoon cream of tartar

GLAZE

- ⅓ cup butter
- 1 teaspoon grated lemon peel
- 2 cups powdered sugar
- 2 to 4 tablespoons fresh lemon juice

1 Move oven rack to lowest position. Heat oven to 325°F. In large bowl, mix flour, granulated sugar, baking powder and salt. Beat in water, oil, vanilla, lemon peel and egg yolks with electric mixer on low speed until smooth.

2 Wash and dry mixer beaters. In large bowl, beat egg whites and cream of tartar with electric mixer on high speed until stiff peaks form. Gradually pour egg yolk mixture over beaten egg whites, folding in with rubber spatula just until blended. Pour into ungreased 10-inch angel food (tube) cake pan.

3 Bake about 1 hour 15 minutes or until top springs back when touched lightly. Immediately turn pan upside down onto heatproof bottle or funnel. Let hang about 2 hours or until cake is completely cool.

4 Loosen sides of cake with knife or long metal spatula; remove from pan.

5 In 1½-quart saucepan, melt butter over low heat; remove from heat. Stir in lemon peel and powdered sugar. Stir in lemon juice, 1 tablespoon at a time, until glaze is smooth and has the consistency of thick syrup. Spread glaze over top of cake, allowing some glaze to drizzle down sides.

1 Serving: Calories 300; Total Fat 12g (Saturated Fat 2.5g, Trans Fat 0g); Cholesterol 125mg; Sodium 360mg; Total Carbohydrate 42g (Dietary Fiber 0g); Protein 6g **Exchanges:** 2 Starch, 1 Other Carbohydrate, 1 Fat **Carbohydrate Choices:** 3

Peach Melba Shortcakes

8 servings • Prep Time: 25 Minutes • Start to Finish: 30 Minutes

FRUIT

3 peaches, peeled and sliced into thin wedges, or 1 bag (1 lb) frozen sliced peaches, thawed

1 container (6 oz) fresh raspberries (1½ cups)

¾ cup granulated sugar

SHORTCAKES

2½ cups all-purpose flour

½ cup granulated sugar

2 teaspoons baking powder

½ teaspoon salt

½ cup cold butter

⅔ cup plus 1 tablespoon milk

½ teaspoon almond extract

1 egg, slightly beaten

¼ cup sliced almonds

3 tablespoons coarse sugar

ICE CREAM

1 pint vanilla ice cream (2 cups)

1 In medium bowl, mix peaches, raspberries and ¾ cup granulated sugar. Let stand so fruit will become juicy.

2 Meanwhile, heat oven to 400°F. In medium bowl, mix flour, ½ cup granulated sugar, baking powder and salt. Cut in butter, using pastry blender or fork, until mixture looks like coarse crumbs. Using wooden spoon, stir in ⅔ cup of the milk, almond extract and egg just until blended. (Dough will be stiff.)

3 On ungreased cookie sheet, drop dough by 8 spoonfuls about 2 inches apart. Brush with remaining 1 tablespoon milk; sprinkle almonds over tops of each. Sprinkle with coarse sugar.

4 Bake 14 to 16 minutes or until light golden brown. Remove from cookie sheet; cool 10 minutes.

5 Cut shortcakes in half. Spoon about ¼ cup ice cream onto bottom of each shortcake. Top each with ½ cup of the peach mixture; add tops of shortcakes.

1 Serving: Calories 520; Total Fat 19g (Saturated Fat 10g, Trans Fat 0.5g); Cholesterol 75mg; Sodium 400mg; Total Carbohydrate 79g (Dietary Fiber 4g); Protein 8g **Exchanges:** 2½ Starch, ½ Fruit, 2 Other Carbohydrate, 3½ Fat **Carbohydrate Choices:** 5

CREAM PUFFS

12 cream puffs • Prep Time: 30 Minutes • Start to Finish: 2 Hours 40 Minutes

PUFFS

½	cup butter, cut into pieces
1	cup water
1	cup all-purpose flour
4	whole eggs

FILLING

⅓	cup granulated sugar
2	tablespoons cornstarch
2	cups milk
2	egg yolks, slightly beaten
2	tablespoons butter, softened
2	teaspoons vanilla

Powdered sugar, if desired

1 Heat oven to 400°F. In 2-quart saucepan, heat ½ cup butter and the water over high heat, stirring occasionally, until boiling rapidly. Stir in flour; reduce heat to low. With wooden spoon, beat vigorously over low heat about 1 minute or until mixture forms a ball; remove from heat.

2 Add eggs, one at a time, beating vigorously with spoon after each addition, until mixture is smooth and glossy.* Onto ungreased cookie sheet, drop dough by slightly less than ¼ cupfuls in mounds about 3 inches apart.

3 Bake 35 to 40 minutes or until puffed and golden. Remove from cookie sheet to cooling rack; prick side of each puff with tip of sharp knife to release steam. Cool away from drafts 30 minutes.

4 Meanwhile, in 2-quart saucepan, stir together granulated sugar and cornstarch with whisk; gradually stir in milk. Cook and stir over medium heat until mixture thickens and boils. Boil and stir 1 minute. Gradually stir at least half of the hot mixture into egg yolks, then stir back into hot mixture in saucepan. Boil and stir 1 minute; remove from heat. Stir in 2 tablespoons butter and the vanilla. Press plastic wrap on surface of filling to prevent skin from forming on top. Refrigerate at least 1 hour or until cool.

5 Using sharp knife, cut off top third of each puff; reserve tops. Pull out any strands of soft dough from puffs. Just before serving, fill bottom of each puff with about 2 rounded tablespoons filling; replace tops. Sprinkle with powdered sugar. Store cream puffs covered in refrigerator.

*Or beat in eggs with electric mixer on medium speed. Beat 1 minute after adding each egg.

1 Cream Puff: Calories 210; Total Fat 13g (Saturated Fat 7g, Trans Fat 0g); Cholesterol 135mg; Sodium 140mg; Total Carbohydrate 17g (Dietary Fiber 0g); Protein 6g **Exchanges:** 1 Starch, ½ Medium-Fat Meat, 2 Fat **Carbohydrate Choices:** 1

Éclairs After dropping dough onto cookie sheet, shape each mound into finger shape, 4½x1½ inch, with metal spatula. Bake and cool as directed. Fill éclairs with filling. Drizzle with a vanilla gaze.

Ice Cream Puffs Omit filling. Fill cream puffs with your favorite flavor ice cream. Cover and freeze until serving. Serve with chocolate, caramel or hot fudge sauce.

Profiteroles Fill cream puffs with filling or ice cream. Drizzle with chocolate sauce.

Refrigerator cookies are loved for their "make-aheadibility." The dough is formed into a log and refrigerated, making it possible to slice and bake as many cookies at a time as you wish!

Orange-Ginger Refrigerator Cookies

6 dozen cookies • Prep Time: 1 Hour 15 Minutes • Start to Finish: 4 Hours 30 Minutes

¾ cup butter, softened

½ cup granulated sugar

½ cup packed brown sugar

1 tablespoon grated orange peel

1 tablespoon orange juice

1 egg

2½ cups all-purpose flour

1 teaspoon baking powder

½ teaspoon salt

½ cup chopped pecans

¼ cup chopped crystallized ginger

¼ cup decorator sugar crystals

1 In large bowl, beat butter, granulated sugar and brown sugar with electric mixer on medium speed until light and fluffy. Beat in orange peel, orange juice and egg until blended. On low speed, beat in flour, baking powder and salt. Stir in pecans and ginger.

2 Divide dough in half. Shape each half into 10-inch log. Sprinkle 2 tablespoons of the sugar crystals on sheet of plastic wrap; roll 1 log in sugar to coat. Wrap log in plastic wrap. Repeat with remaining log and sugar crystals. Refrigerate about 3 hours or until very firm.

3 Heat oven to 375°F. Cut logs into ¼-inch slices. On ungreased cookie sheets, place slices 2 inches apart.

4 Bake 8 to 10 minutes or until edges start to brown and tops are light golden brown. Immediately remove from cookie sheets to cooling racks. Cool completely, about 15 minutes.

1 Cookie: Calories 60; Total Fat 2.5g (Saturated Fat 1.5g, Trans Fat 0g); Cholesterol 10mg; Sodium 40mg; Total Carbohydrate 8g (Dietary Fiber 0g); Protein 0g **Exchanges:** ½ Other Carbohydrate, ½ Fat **Carbohydrate Choices:** ½

BETTY'S KITCHEN TIPS

These crisp, delicious cookies would be a welcome holiday treat. Stack 6 or 8 cookies, and tie with a pretty ribbon to present as a small gift.

For a special presentation, melt about ⅔ cup semisweet or milk chocolate chips in a long, narrow microwavable dish, such as a butter dish. Dip about ¼ inch of one edge of each cookie into chocolate; place on waxed paper and let stand about 40 minutes or until chocolate is set.

Food stylist Cindy Lund first made these cookies with her two children when they were just two and four years old. She shaped the dough into balls, and the kids rolled them in sugar. They even mailed a batch to Grandma and Grandpa. Cindy says, "They're easy to make, taste great and travel well, too."

MOLASSES CRINKLES

About 3 dozen cookies • Prep Time: 45 Minutes • Start to Finish: 1 Hour 45 Minutes

1 cup packed brown sugar

½ cup butter, softened

¼ cup shortening

¼ cup molasses

1 egg

2 cups all-purpose flour

2 teaspoons baking soda

1 teaspoon ground cinnamon

1 teaspoon ground ginger

½ teaspoon ground cloves

¼ teaspoon salt

Granulated sugar

1. In large bowl, mix brown sugar, butter, shortening, molasses and egg until well blended. Stir in remaining ingredients except granulated sugar. Cover and refrigerate at least 1 hour until chilled.

2. Heat oven to 375°F. Shape dough into 1¼-inch balls; roll in granulated sugar. Place about 2 inches apart on ungreased cookie sheet. Bake 10 to 11 minutes or just until set. Cool slightly; remove from cookie sheet. Cool on wire rack.

1 Cookie: Calories 110; Total Fat 4g (Saturated Fat 2g, Trans Fat 0g); Cholesterol 10mg; Sodium 110mg; Total Carbohydrate 16g (Dietary Fiber 0g); Protein 1g **Exchanges:** 1 Other Carbohydrate, 1 Fat **Carbohydrate Choices:** 1

BLAST FROM THE PAST:

(*Betty Crocker Picture Cook Book*, 1950)
Cookie Storage

Store cooled cookies properly to keep top eating quality. Keep crisp, thin cookies in can with loose cover.

Keep soft cookies in airtight container (a covered earthen jar or a can with tight cover). Slices of apple or orange in jar help mellow and moisten cookies. Change fruit frequently.

CHERRY BLINKS

About 3 dozen cookies • Prep Time: 40 Minutes • Start to Finish: 40 Minutes

1¾ cups Wheaties cereal

½ cup sugar

⅓ cup shortening

1½ tablespoons milk

1 teaspoon vanilla

1 egg

1 cup all-purpose flour

½ teaspoon baking powder

¼ teaspoon baking soda

¼ teaspoon salt

½ cup raisins

½ cup chopped nuts

About 36 candied or maraschino cherries

1 Heat oven to 375°F. Crush cereal; set aside. In large bowl, mix sugar, shortening, milk, vanilla and egg. Stir in flour, baking powder, baking soda and salt. Stir in raisins and nuts.

2 Drop dough by teaspoonfuls into crushed cereal; roll gently until completely coated. Place cookies about 2 inches apart on ungreased cookie sheet. Press cherry into each cookie.

3 Bake 10 to 12 minutes or just until set. Immediately remove from cookie sheet to wire rack.

1 Cookie: Calories 80; Total Fat 3g (Saturated Fat 0.5g, Trans Fat 0g); Cholesterol 5mg; Sodium 45mg; Total Carbohydrate 11g (Dietary Fiber 0g); Protein 1g
Exchanges: 1 Other Carbohydrate, ½ Fat **Carbohydrate Choices:** 1

HERMITS

About 3 dozen cookies • Prep Time: 10 Minutes • Start to Finish: 40 Minutes

1 cup packed brown sugar
¼ cup shortening
¼ cup butter, softened
¼ cup cold coffee
1 egg
1¾ cups all-purpose flour
½ teaspoon baking soda
½ teaspoon ground nutmeg
½ teaspoon ground cinnamon
¼ teaspoon salt
¾ cup raisins
½ cup chopped nuts

1 Heat oven to 375°F.

2 In medium bowl, mix brown sugar, shortening, butter, coffee and egg. Stir in flour, baking soda, nutmeg, cinnamon and salt. Stir in raisins and nuts.

3 Drop dough by rounded teaspoonfuls about 2 inches apart onto ungreased cookie sheet.

4 Bake 8 to 10 minutes or until almost no indentation remains when touched in center. Cool slightly; remove from cookie sheet. Cool on wire rack.

1 Serving: Calories 90; Total Fat 4g (Saturated Fat 1.5g, Trans Fat 0g); Cholesterol 10mg; Sodium 50mg; Total Carbohydrate 13g (Dietary Fiber 0g); Protein 1g
Exchanges: 1 Other Carbohydrate, 1 Fat **Carbohydrate Choices:** 1

DIVINITY

About 30 candies • Prep Time: 30 Minutes • Start to Finish: 1 Hour

2 egg whites

½ cup water

⅓ cup light corn syrup

2 cups sugar

¼ teaspoon salt, if desired

1 teaspoon vanilla

½ cup chopped nuts

1 Line large cookie sheet with waxed paper. In large bowl, beat egg whites with electric mixer on high speed until soft peaks form; set aside.

2 In 3-quart saucepan, mix water, corn syrup, sugar and salt. Cook over medium heat, stirring constantly, until sugar is dissolved. Without stirring, cook 8 to 10 minutes or until syrup reaches 250°F on candy thermometer.

3 When syrup is 250°F, continue beating egg whites on high speed while slowly pouring syrup into egg whites. Beat 2 to 3 minutes or until mixture holds a soft peak and does not flatten when dropped from a spoon.

4 Fold in vanilla and nuts. Quickly spoon mixture by rounded teaspoonfuls onto cookie sheet. Let stand about 30 minutes or until completely set.

1 Candy: Calories 80; Total Fat 1.5g (Saturated Fat 0g, Trans Fat 0g); Cholesterol 0mg; Sodium 5mg; Total Carbohydrate 17g (Dietary Fiber 0g); Protein 0g
Exchanges: 1 Other Carbohydrate, ½ Fat **Carbohydrate Choices:** 1

Date Bars

36 bars • Prep Time: 30 Minutes • Start to Finish: 1 Hour 5 Minutes

DATE FILLING

3   cups chopped pitted dates (1 lb)

1½   cups water

¼   cup granulated sugar

BARS

1   cup packed brown sugar

1   cup butter, softened

1¾   cups all-purpose or whole wheat flour

1½   cups quick-cooking oats

½   teaspoon baking soda

½   teaspoon salt

1   In 2-quart saucepan, cook filling ingredients over low heat about 10 minutes, stirring constantly, until thickened. Cool 5 minutes.

2   Heat oven to 400°F. Grease bottom and sides of 13x9-inch pan with shortening.

3   In large bowl, stir together brown sugar and butter until well mixed. Stir in flour, oats, baking soda and salt until crumbly. Press half of the crumb mixture evenly in bottom of pan. Spread with filling. Top with remaining crumb mixture; press lightly.

4   Bake 25 to 30 minutes or until light brown. Cool 5 minutes in pan on cooling rack. Cut into 6 rows by 6 columns while warm.

1 Bar: Calories 150; Total Fat 5g (Saturated Fat 3.5g, Trans Fat 0g); Cholesterol 15mg; Sodium 105mg; Total Carbohydrate 23g (Dietary Fiber 1g); Protein 1g **Exchanges:** ½ Starch, 1 Other Carbohydrate, 1 Fat **Carbohydrate Choices:** 1½

BANANA CREAM PIE

8 servings • Prep Time: 30 Minutes • Start to Finish: 2 Hours 30 Minutes

PASTRY

1	cup plus 1 tablespoon all-purpose flour
½	teaspoon salt
⅓	cup cold shortening
3	to 5 tablespoons ice-cold water

FILLING

4	egg yolks
⅔	cup sugar
¼	cup cornstarch
½	teaspoon salt
3	cups milk
2	tablespoons butter, softened
2	teaspoons vanilla
2	large ripe but firm bananas

Sweetened whipped cream (page 184), if desired

1   In medium bowl, mix flour and ½ teaspoon salt. Cut in shortening, using pastry blender or fork, until mixture forms coarse crumbs the size of small peas. Sprinkle with water, 1 tablespoon at a time, tossing with fork until all flour is moistened and pastry almost leaves sides of bowl. (Add 1 to 2 teaspoons more water if necessary.)

2   Gather pastry into a ball. Shape into flattened round on lightly floured surface. Wrap flattened round in plastic wrap and refrigerate 45 minutes or until dough is firm and cold, yet pliable.

3   Heat oven to 450°F. Using floured rolling pin, roll pastry on lightly floured surface into 11-inch round. Carefully place pasty in 9-inch glass pie plate. Bake 8 to 10 minutes or until light golden brown. Cool completely.

4   Meanwhile, in medium bowl, beat egg yolks with fork; set aside. In 2-quart saucepan, mix sugar, cornstarch and salt. Gradually stir in milk. Cook over medium heat, stirring constantly, until mixture thickens and boils. Boil and stir 1 minute. Immediately stir at least half of hot mixture gradually into egg yolks, then stir back into hot mixture in saucepan. Boil and stir 1 minute; remove from heat. Stir in butter and vanilla; cool filling slightly.

5   Slice bananas into cooled baked crust; pour warm filling over bananas. Press plastic wrap on filling to prevent a skin from forming on top. Refrigerate at least 2 hours or until set. Remove plastic wrap. Top pie with whipped cream. Store covered in refrigerator.

1 Serving: Calories 410; Total Fat 22g (Saturated Fat 8g, Trans Fat 2g); Cholesterol 135mg; Sodium 370mg; Total Carbohydrate 46g (Dietary Fiber 1g); Protein 7g **Exchanges:** 1 Starch, 1 Fruit, ½ Other Carbohydrate, ½ Low-Fat Milk, 4½ Fat **Carbohydrate Choices:** 3

Butterscotch Cream Pie Substitute packed dark or light brown sugar for the granulated sugar. Omit bananas.

Chocolate-Banana Cream Pie Make Chocolate Cream Pie filling (below). Cool slightly. Slice 2 large ripe but firm bananas into cooled baked crust; pour warm filling over bananas. Continue as directed.

Chocolate Cream Pie Increase sugar to 1½ cups and cornstarch to ⅓ cup; omit butter and bananas. Stir in 2 oz unsweetened baking chocolate, chopped, after stirring in milk.

Coconut Cream Pie Increase cornstarch to ⅓ cup. Substitute 1 can (14 oz) coconut milk (not cream of coconut) and milk to equal 3 cups for the milk. Stir in ¾ cup toasted coconut with the butter. Omit bananas. Refrigerate pie 3 hours or until set. Top with whipped cream; sprinkle with ¼ cup toasted coconut.

Triple-Threat Coconut Cream Pie

8 servings • Prep Time: 40 Minutes • Start to Finish: 3 Hours 45 Minutes

1 refrigerated pie crust, softened as directed on box

1 can (13.5 oz) coconut milk, shaken well

½ cup plus 1 tablespoon sweetened shredded or flaked coconut, toasted

1 cup whole milk

½ vanilla bean, split (or 1 teaspoon vanilla)

⅔ cup sugar

¼ teaspoon salt

5 large egg yolks

¼ cup cornstarch

½ teaspoon coconut extract

2 tablespoons unsalted butter, cut into 4 pieces

TOPPING

1½ cups heavy whipping cream, well chilled

1½ tablespoons sugar

2 teaspoons dark rum (or 1 teaspoon vanilla)

¼ cup sweetened shredded or flaked coconut, toasted

1 oz white chocolate, shaved

1 Heat oven to 450°F.

2 Unroll pie crust onto cooking parchment or waxed paper. Brush a small amount of coconut milk onto dough (just enough to moisten it). Sprinkle ½ tablespoon of the toasted coconut evenly on dough, then press it lightly into dough, just enough to make it stick.

3 Sprinkle ½ tablespoon toasted coconut onto bottom of 9-inch pie plate, then fit dough into plate. Prick bottom and sides with fork. Bake 10 to 12 minutes or until light brown. Cool.

4 Bring remaining coconut milk, whole milk, remaining ½ cup toasted coconut, vanilla bean, ⅓ cup of the sugar and the salt to a simmer in 2-quart saucepan over medium heat, stirring occasionally with wooden spoon, about 5 minutes to dissolve sugar.

5 In a separate large bowl, with whisk, beat egg yolks, remaining ⅓ cup sugar and cornstarch until well combined. Gradually beat simmering liquid into yolk mixture to temper it, then return entire mixture to saucepan, scraping bowl with rubber spatula. Discard vanilla bean.

6 Bring mixture to a simmer over medium heat, beating constantly with whisk, 5 to 6 minutes or until mixture is thickened.

7 Remove from heat; beat in coconut extract and butter. Pour into cooled crust; press a sheet of plastic wrap directly onto the surface of filling and refrigerate until filling is cold and firm, at least 3 hours or overnight.

8   Just before serving, beat cream and 1½ tablespoons sugar in a chilled bowl using electric mixer at medium speed until soft peaks form. Add rum and continue to beat until slightly stiff peaks form. Spread or pipe whipped cream over chilled filling. Sprinkle ¼ cup toasted coconut and shaved chocolate over the top. Store in refrigerator.

1 Serving: Calories 580; Total Fat 41g (Saturated Fat 27g, Trans Fat 0.5g); Cholesterol 190mg; Sodium 270mg; Total Carbohydrate 47g (Dietary Fiber 1g); Protein 5g **Exchanges:** 1½ Starch, 1½ Other Carbohydrate, 8 Fat
Carbohydrate Choices: 3

BETTY'S KITCHEN TIP

After opening, bagged coconut is best stored for only up to 6 months.

FOOD AND FIRE OBSESSION

Foods lit on fire—the pinnacle of food presentation—seemed to begin with dessert. By the mid-1950s, flambéed desserts such as French Crepes Suzette (page 212), Bananas Foster (page 216) and Ultimate Cherries Jubilee (page 215) were very popular. This dramatic presentation style involves igniting warmed liquor in a dish just before serving. Mostly it's about the show, but a side benefit is that some of the alcohol burns off, leaving the essence to add flavor to the dish.

Today, serving one of these foods will make a memorable event—bringing oohs and aahs. Dim the lights just enough to see the flame, while having enough light to still safely see what you are doing. Here's how to do it safely and successfully:

1. Have all your equipment and ingredients prepped before you are ready to ignite the dish. Pull long hair and sleeves back.

2. Liquor should be at least 80 proof (40% alcohol). Liquor that is 120 proof or higher is highly flammable and is not recommended for igniting as it could combust in a very unsafe manner. Use caution—do not carry a dish that's flaming.

3. Liquor needs to be warm in order to ignite. Use a pan on the stove to warm the liquid just until steam rises from it or small bubbles form along the edge. Once the liquor is warm, immediately add it to the dish and ignite.

4. Use a serving cart away from the table and flammable objects and a cordless portable burner to allow your guests to watch you ignite the food. Keep a large metal pan lid on hand to distinguish the flames, should they get too big.

5. Never pour liquor from a bottle that's near an open flame (the flame can follow the liquor stream back into the bottle and explode). Always remove the pan (where the hot liquor will be added) from the heat source before adding the liquor to avoid burning yourself.

6. Always ignite with a long match and at the fumes at the edge of the pan—not the liquid itself. Do not tip the pan to ignite from the burner. Never lean over the pan as you ignite.

7. Let the flame burn itself out—it usually only burns for a small amount of time.

8. Practice before your guests arrive, to be sure you have the technique mastered.

BLAST FROM THE PAST:

(*Betty Crocker Picture Cook Book*, 1950)
Flaming Cabbage

Clean a large cabbage. Curl outer leaves back from top. Cut out center; hollow it out about 6 inches deep. Place a can of cooking fuel in the cavity (lamp hidden, but flame should come almost to the top of the cabbage). Place cabbage on serving plate. Surround with a frill of parsley. Push wooden picks through cocktail sausages, and stick into the cabbage. Stick an olive onto end of each (to protect fingers from flame). Guests broil their own sausages.

French Crepes Suzette

6 servings • Prep Time: 35 Minutes • Start to Finish: 35 Minutes

1 cup Original Bisquick mix

¾ cup milk

2 eggs

¼ cup butter

1 teaspoon grated orange peel

¼ cup orange juice

⅓ cup sugar

¼ cup orange-flavored liqueur

Additional orange peel, if desired

1 In small bowl, beat Bisquick mix, milk and eggs with fork or whisk until blended. Lightly butter 8-inch skillet; heat over medium heat until bubbly.

2 For each crepe, pour 2 tablespoons of the batter into skillet; immediately rotate skillet until batter covers bottom. Cook until golden brown. Run wide metal spatula around edge to loosen; turn and cook other side until golden brown. Stack crepes, placing waxed paper between each; keep covered.

3 In 10-inch skillet, heat ¼ cup butter, orange peel, orange juice and sugar to boiling, stirring occasionally. Reduce heat; simmer uncovered 5 minutes, stirring occasionally. In 1-quart saucepan, heat liqueur but do not boil.

4 Fold crepes into fourths; place in hot orange sauce in skillet and turn once. Arrange crepes around edge of skillet. Pour warm liqueur into center of skillet and carefully ignite. After flame dies, place 2 crepes on each dessert plate; spoon warm sauce onto crepes. Garnish with additional orange peel.

1 Serving: Calories 270; Total Fat 13g (Saturated Fat 7g, Trans Fat 1g); Cholesterol 95mg; Sodium 330mg; Total Carbohydrate 30g (Dietary Fiber 0g); Protein 4g
Exchanges: 1 Starch, 1 Other Carbohydrate, 2½ Fat **Carbohydrate Choices:** 2

Ultimate Cherries Jubilee

6 servings • Prep Time: 25 Minutes • Start to Finish: 25 Minutes

¼ cup sugar

1 tablespoon cornstarch

Dash salt

⅓ cup water

1½ cups sweet cherries, pitted, halved

¼ cup kirsch liqueur or ½ teaspoon almond extract

6 brownies (2½x2½ inches each)

1 pint vanilla ice cream (2 cups)

1 In small skillet, combine sugar, cornstarch, salt and water. Cook over medium heat until mixture thickens, stirring constantly. Stir in cherries. Reduce heat to low; cook 3 to 5 minutes, stirring occasionally. Remove from heat; stir in kirsch.*

2 To serve, place brownies on individual dessert plates. Top each with ⅓ cup ice cream. Spoon warm cherry sauce over ice cream. Serve immediately.

*To flame dessert, omit kirsch from sauce. Just before serving, top brownies with ice cream. Place kirsch in small long-handled pan; heat just until warm. Pour warm kirsch over cherry sauce; ignite immediately. Once flame goes out, spoon cherry sauce over ice cream.

1 Serving: Calories 380; Total Fat 16g (Saturated Fat 10g, Trans Fat 0g); Cholesterol 65mg; Sodium 125mg; Total Carbohydrate 53g (Dietary Fiber 2g); Protein 4g **Exchanges:** ½ Starch, 2½ Other Carbohydrate, ½ Milk, 2½ Fat **Carbohydrate Choices:** 3½

Bananas Foster

6 servings • Prep Time: 20 Minutes • Start to Finish: 20 Minutes

2   tablespoons lemon juice

4   bananas, cut into thirds, cut
     in half lengthwise

½   cup butter

¾   cup firmly packed
     brown sugar

¼   teaspoon ground cinnamon

¼   cup crème de banana
     liqueur

¼   cup dark rum, warmed*

1½   pints vanilla ice cream
     (3 cups)

18   pecan halves, lightly
     toasted**

1 Place lemon juice in shallow bowl. Dip each banana piece
in lemon juice; set aside. In large skillet over low heat, melt
butter. Add sugar, cinnamon and crème de banana; stir
constantly 3 to 4 minutes or until sugar is dissolved. Stir in
banana pieces; cook 2 minutes.

2 Remove from heat. Pour warm rum over top of banana
mixture; do not stir. Tilt pan slightly to pool rum; ignite.
Spoon sauce over bananas until flame dies out.

3 To serve, divide warm bananas evenly among 6 individual
dessert plates. Top each serving with ½ cup ice cream. Spoon
sauce evenly over ice cream and bananas; garnish with
3 pecan halves. Serve immediately.

*Warm rum in a small saucepan over very low heat. DO NOT HEAT
IN MICROWAVE.

**To toast pecans, spread on cookie sheet; bake at 350°F 5 to 7 minutes
or until golden brown, stirring occasionally.

1 Serving: Calories 510; Total Fat 26g (Saturated Fat 15g, Trans Fat 1g);
Cholesterol 70mg; Sodium 180mg; Total Carbohydrate 62g (Dietary Fiber 3g);
Protein 3g **Exchanges:** ½ Fruit, 3½ Other Carbohydrate, ½ Milk, 4½ Fat
Carbohydrate Choices: 4

White Ting-a-Lings

12 oz vanilla-flavored candy coating or almond bark, cut into pieces

1½ cups chow mein noodles

1 cup salted peanuts

1 Line cookie sheet with waxed paper. In 2-quart saucepan, melt candy coating over low heat, stirring constantly.

2 Stir in chow mein noodles and peanuts. Drop by teaspoonfuls onto cookie sheet. Let stand until set. Store in refrigerator.

1 Candy: Calories 90; Total Fat 6g (Saturated Fat 3g, Trans Fat 0g); Cholesterol 0mg; Sodium 40mg; Total Carbohydrate 8g (Dietary Fiber 0g); Protein 1g **Exchanges:** ½ Starch, 1 Fat **Carbohydrate Choices:** ½

Although we are not sure where this fun recipe originated, we do know that the candies are always popular and disappear quickly!

Lemon Schaum Torte

8 servings • Prep Time: 35 Minutes • Start to Finish: 17 Hours 5 Minutes

MERINGUE SHELL

3	egg whites
¼	teaspoon cream of tartar
¾	cup sugar

FILLING AND TOPPING

¾	cup sugar
3	tablespoons cornstarch
¼	teaspoon salt
¾	cup water
3	egg yolks, slightly beaten
1	tablespoon butter
1	teaspoon grated lemon peel
⅓	cup lemon juice
1	cup whipping cream
1	package (6 oz) fresh raspberries

1 Heat oven to 275°F. Line cookie sheet with cooking parchment paper. In medium bowl, beat egg whites and cream of tartar with electric mixer on high speed until foamy. Beat in ¾ cup sugar, 1 tablespoon at a time; continue beating until stiff peaks form and mixture is glossy. Do not underbeat. On cookie sheet, shape meringue into 9-inch round with back of spoon, building up sides.

2 Bake 1 hour 30 minutes. Turn off oven; leave meringue in oven with door closed 1 hour. Finish cooling at room temperature, about 2 hours.

3 In 2-quart saucepan, mix ¾ cup sugar, cornstarch and salt. Gradually stir in water. Cook over medium heat, stirring constantly, until mixture thickens and boils. Boil and stir 1 minute. Gradually stir at least half of the hot mixture into egg yolks; stir back into hot mixture in saucepan. Boil and stir 1 minute; remove from heat.

4 Stir in butter, lemon peel and lemon juice. Press plastic wrap onto surface to keep it from drying out. Cool to room temperature. Spoon into meringue shell. Cover and refrigerate at least 12 hours but no longer than 24 hours.

5 In chilled medium bowl, beat whipping cream with electric mixer on high speed until soft peaks form. Spread over filling. Refrigerate until serving. Garnish with raspberries. Store in refrigerator.

1 Serving: Calories 300; Total Fat 13g (Saturated Fat 7g, Trans Fat 0g); Cholesterol 105mg; Sodium 120mg; Total Carbohydrate 45g (Dietary Fiber 1g); Protein 3g **Exchanges:** 1 Starch, 2 Other Carbohydrate, 2½ Fat **Carbohydrate Choices:** 3

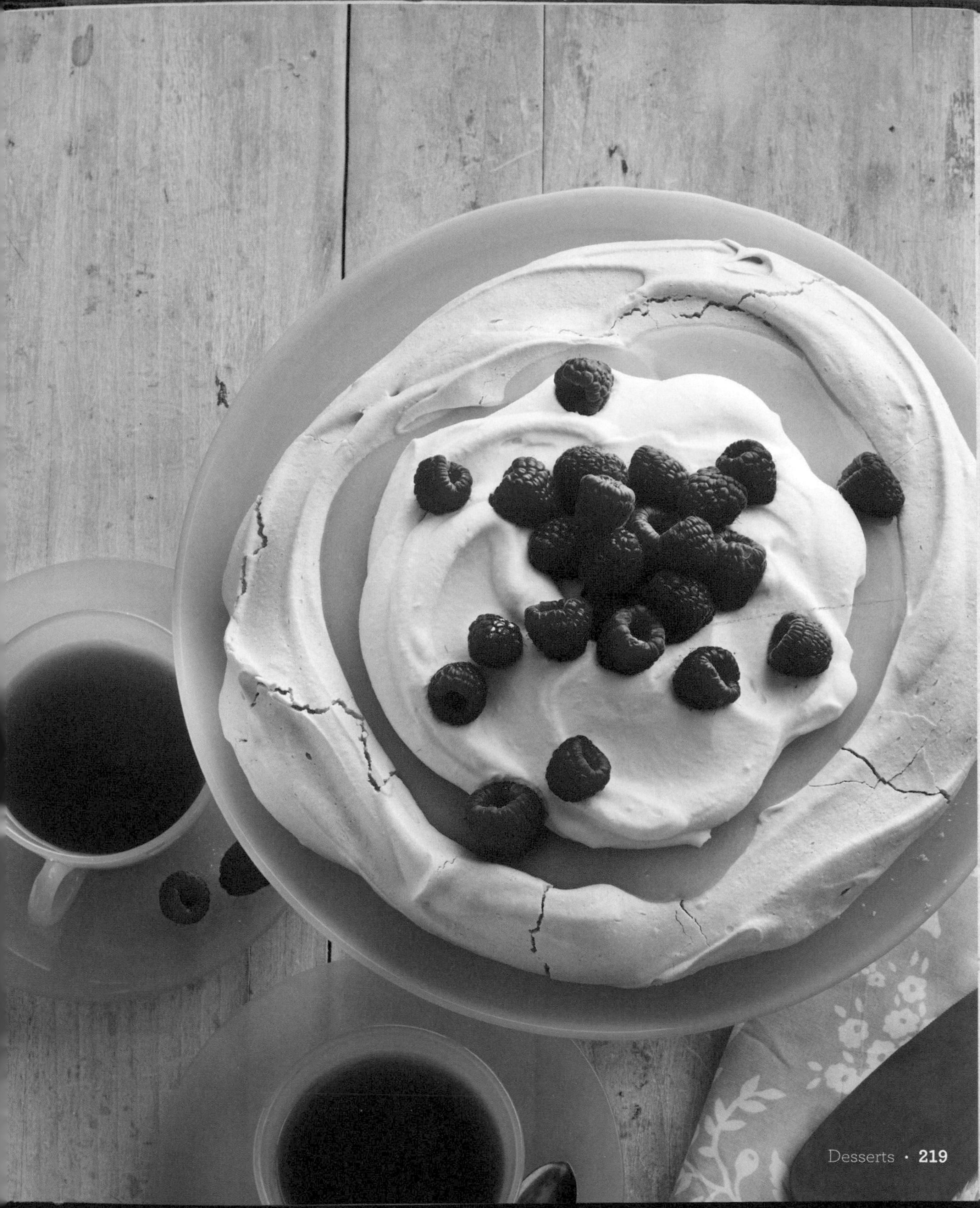

A "cloud" of meringue is heavenly when filled with a cream cheese blend and colorful, sweet-tart fruit.

CHERRY BERRIES ON A CLOUD

10 servings • Prep Time: 20 Minutes • Start to Finish: 25 Hours 20 Minutes

MERINGUE

- 6 egg whites
- ½ teaspoon cream of tartar
- ¼ teaspoon salt
- 1¾ cups sugar

FILLING

- 2 packages (3 oz each) cream cheese, softened
- 1 cup sugar
- 1 teaspoon vanilla
- 2 cups whipping cream
- 2 cups miniature marshmallows

CHERRY-BERRY TOPPING

- 1 can (21 oz) cherry pie filling
- 1 teaspoon lemon juice
- 2 cups sliced strawberries or 1 package (16 oz) frozen strawberries, thawed, drained

1 Heat oven to 275°F. Grease bottom and sides of 13x9-inch pan. In large bowl, beat egg whites, cream of tartar and salt with electric mixer on high speed until foamy. Beat in 1¾ cups sugar, 1 tablespoon at a time; continue beating until stiff and glossy. Do not underbeat. Spread in pan.

2 Bake 1 hour. Turn off oven; leave meringue in oven with door closed 12 hours.

3 In large bowl, mix cream cheese, 1 cup sugar and vanilla until smooth. In chilled medium bowl, beat whipping cream until stiff peaks form. Fold whipped cream and marshmallows into cream cheese mixture. Spread evenly over meringue. Refrigerate at least 12 hours but no longer than 24 hours.

4 In medium bowl, mix all topping ingredients until well blended. Spoon over individual servings of dessert. Store in refrigerator.

1 Serving: Calories 540; Total Fat 21g (Saturated Fat 13g, Trans Fat 0.5g); Cholesterol 70mg; Sodium 190mg; Total Carbohydrate 83g (Dietary Fiber 0g); Protein 4g **Exchanges:** ½ Fruit, 5 Other Carbohydrate, ½ Very Lean Meat, 4 Fat **Carbohydrate Choices:** 5½

Peach Cobbler

6 servings • Prep Time: 25 Minutes • Start to Finish: 50 Minutes

⅓ cup plus 2 tablespoons
    sugar

1 tablespoon cornstarch

¼ teaspoon ground cinnamon

6 peaches, peeled, cut into
    ½-inch slices (6 cups)

2 tablespoons water

2 teaspoons lemon juice

1 cup Original Bisquick mix

⅓ cup milk

1 tablespoon butter, melted

Sweetened Whipped Cream
(page 184), if desired

1. Heat oven to 400°F. In 4-quart saucepan, mix ⅓ cup of the sugar, the cornstarch and cinnamon. Stir in peaches, water and lemon juice. Heat to boiling, stirring constantly; boil and stir 1 minute. Pour into ungreased 8- or 9-inch square (2-quart) glass baking dish.

2. In medium bowl, stir Bisquick mix, 1 tablespoon of the sugar, the milk and melted butter until soft dough forms.

3. Drop dough in 6 tablespoonfuls onto hot peach mixture. Sprinkle remaining 1 tablespoon sugar over dough.

4. Bake 20 to 25 minutes or until golden brown. Serve with whipped cream.

1 Serving: Calories 240; Total Fat 5g (Saturated Fat 2g, Trans Fat 1g); Cholesterol 5mg; Sodium 260mg; Total Carbohydrate 45g (Dietary Fiber 3g); Protein 3g **Exchanges:** 1 Starch, 1 Fruit, 1 Other Carbohydrate, 1 Fat **Carbohydrate Choices:** 3

RICE PUDDING

8 servings • Prep Time: 15 Minutes • Start to Finish: 1 Hour 30 Minutes

½ cup uncooked long-grain white rice

1 cup water

2 whole eggs or 4 egg yolks

½ cup sugar

½ cup raisins or chopped dried apricots

2½ cups milk

1 teaspoon vanilla

¼ teaspoon salt

Ground cinnamon or nutmeg

Raspberry Sauce (right) or Sweetened Whipped Cream (page 184), if desired

1 In 1½-quart saucepan, heat rice and water to boiling, stirring once or twice; reduce heat to low. Cover and simmer 14 minutes (do not lift cover or stir). All water should be absorbed; if not, drain excess water.

2 Heat oven to 325°F. In ungreased 1½-quart casserole, beat eggs with whisk or fork. Stir in sugar, raisins, milk, vanilla, salt and hot rice. Sprinkle with cinnamon.

3 Bake uncovered 45 minutes, stirring every 15 minutes. Top of pudding will be very wet and not set (overbaking may cause pudding to curdle).

4 Stir well; let stand 15 minutes. Enough liquid will be absorbed while standing to make pudding creamy. Serve warm, or cover and refrigerate about 3 hours or until chilled. Serve with Raspberry Sauce. Store covered in refrigerator.

1 Serving: Calories 180; Total Fat 3g (Saturated Fat 1g, Trans Fat 0g); Cholesterol 60mg; Sodium 125mg; Total Carbohydrate 33g (Dietary Fiber 0g); Protein 5g **Exchanges:** 2 Starch, ½ Fat **Carbohydrate Choices:** 2

Raspberry Sauce In 1-quart saucepan, mix 3 tablespoons sugar and 2 teaspoons cornstarch. Stir in ⅓ cup water and 1 package (10 oz) thawed frozen raspberries in syrup. Cook over medium heat, stirring constantly, until mixture boils. Boil and stir 1 minute. Strain sauce through fine-mesh strainer, if desired. Serve warm or cool.

The classic Southern Hummingbird Cake is banana-pineapple spice cake that is also known as "cake that doesn't last." We've added fun twists of the Bundt shape and making it an upside-down cake as well.

HUMMINGBIRD UPSIDE-DOWN POKE BUNDT CAKE

14 servings • Prep Time: 35 Minutes • Start to Finish: 3 Hours 35 Minutes

CAKE

- ½ cup plus 2 tablespoons butter, melted
- ⅓ cup packed brown sugar
- 6 pineapple slices (from 20-oz can), drained, juice reserved
- 1 box Betty Crocker™ SuperMoist™ yellow cake mix
- ½ cup reserved pineapple juice
- 3 eggs
- 1 cup mashed very ripe bananas (2 medium)
- 1½ teaspoons ground cinnamon
- ½ teaspoon ground nutmeg

FILLING

- 1 cup (from 14-oz can) canned sweetened condensed milk (not evaporated)
- ¼ cup reserved pineapple juice

TOPPING

- ½ cup powdered sugar
- 2 teaspoons reserved pineapple juice
- 2 tablespoons chopped pecans, toasted*

1 Heat oven to 350°F. Generously spray 12-cup Bundt cake pan with baking spray with flour. Pour 2 tablespoons of the melted butter evenly in bottom of pan. Sprinkle brown sugar over butter. Cut pineapple slices in half. Line bottom of pan with pineapple halves, fitting slices close together. Set aside.

2 In large bowl, beat cake mix, remaining ½ cup melted butter, ½ cup reserved pineapple juice, eggs, bananas, cinnamon and nutmeg with electric mixer on medium speed 2 minutes. Pour into pan over pineapple. Bake 40 to 45 minutes or until toothpick inserted in center comes out clean. Remove from oven; cool 15 minutes.

3 In small bowl, mix filling ingredients. With handle of wooden spoon (¼ to ½ inch in diameter), poke holes halfway down in cake every inch, wiping spoon handle occasionally to prevent sticking. Carefully pour filling mixture over holes in cake, using spoon to direct mixture into holes. Refrigerate in pan uncovered 2 hours.

4 Remove from refrigerator and run metal spatula around outer and inside edges of pan to loosen cake; turn upside down onto serving platter. In small bowl, mix powdered sugar and 2 teaspoons reserved pineapple juice. Drizzle on top of cake; sprinkle with pecans.

*To toast pecans, sprinkle in ungreased heavy skillet. Cook over medium-low heat 5 to 7 minutes, stirring frequently until browning begins, then stirring constantly until golden brown.

1 Serving: Calories 360; Total Fat 13g (Saturated Fat 8g, Trans Fat 0g); Cholesterol 70mg; Sodium 330mg; Total Carbohydrate 55g (Dietary Fiber 1g); Protein 4g
Exchanges: 1 Starch, 2½ Other Carbohydrate, 2½ Fat **Carbohydrate Choices:** 3½

BETTY'S KITCHEN TIP

It is very important to use baking spray with flour for coating the pan. It will help with successful removal from the pan.

Daffodil

Pink Azalea

Delicious display of cakes
from Betty Crocker's 1950
Picture Cook Book

Old
Kentucky

Brown-Eyed Susan

Chocolate Joy

Bouquet of Flowers

METRIC CONVERSION GUIDE

VOLUME

U.S. Units	Canadian Metric	Australian Metric
¼ teaspoon	1 mL	1 ml
½ teaspoon	2 mL	2 ml
1 teaspoon	5 mL	5 ml
1 tablespoon	15 mL	20 ml
¼ cup	50 mL	60 ml
⅓ cup	75 mL	80 ml
½ cup	125 mL	125 ml
⅔ cup	150 mL	170 ml
¾ cup	175 mL	190 ml
1 cup	250 mL	250 ml
1 quart	1 liter	1 liter
1½ quarts	1.5 liters	1.5 liters
2 quarts	2 liters	2 liters
2½ quarts	2.5 liters	2.5 liters
3 quarts	3 liters	3 liters
4 quarts	4 liters	4 liters

WEIGHT

U.S. Units	Canadian Metric	Australian Metric
1 ounce	30 grams	30 grams
2 ounces	55 grams	60 grams
3 ounces	85 grams	90 grams
4 ounces (¼ pound)	115 grams	125 grams
8 ounces (½ pound)	225 grams	225 grams
16 ounces (1 pound)	455 grams	500 grams
1 pound	455 grams	0.5 kilogram

Note: The recipes in this cookbook have not been developed or tested using metric measures. When converting recipes to metric, some variations in quality may be noted.

MEASUREMENTS

Inches	Centimeters
1	2.5
2	5.0
3	7.5
4	10.0
5	12.5
6	15.0
7	17.5
8	20.5
9	23.0
10	25.5
11	28.0
12	30.5
13	33.0

TEMPERATURES

Fahrenheit	Celsius
32°	0°
212°	100°
250°	120°
275°	140°
300°	150°
325°	160°
350°	180°
375°	190°
400°	200°
425°	220°
450°	230°
475°	240°
500°	260°

RECIPE TESTING AND CALCULATING NUTRITION INFORMATION

RECIPE TESTING:

- Large eggs and 2% milk were used unless otherwise indicated.

- Fat-free, low-fat, low-sodium or lite products were not used unless indicated.

- No nonstick cookware and bakeware were used unless otherwise indicated. No dark-colored, black or insulated bakeware was used.

- When a pan is specified, a metal pan was used; a baking dish or pie plate means ovenproof glass was used.

- An electric hand mixer was used for mixing only when mixer speeds are specified.

CALCULATING NUTRITION:

- The first ingredient was used wherever a choice is given, such as ⅓ cup sour cream or plain yogurt.

- The first amount was used wherever a range is given, such as 3- to 3½-pound whole chicken.

- The first serving number was used wherever a range is given, such as 4 to 6 servings.

- "If desired" ingredients were not included.

- Only the amount of a marinade or frying oil that is absorbed was included.

- Diabetic exchanges are not calculated in recipies containing uncooked alcohol due to its effect on blood sugar levels.

INDEX

Page numbers in *italics* indicate
illustrations

A

Almonds
Chicken Curry Spread, 33
Danish Puff, *116*, 117
Hot Crab Dip, *30*, 31
and Mushrooms, Wild Rice with, 163
Peach Melba Shortcakes, *192*, 193
Sugared, Mandarin Salad with, 152, *153*

Anadama Bread, *134*, 135

Appetizers & snacks
Cheese Ball, *26*, 27
Chicken Curry Spread, 33
Classic Shrimp Cocktail, 22, *23*
Creamy Shrimp Appetizers, 32
Deluxe Deviled Eggs; variations, 18–19, *19*
Frosted Liverwurst Pâté, 38
Havarti-Cheddar Fondue, *34*, 35
Nutty Caramel Corn, 36, *37*
Hot Crab Dip, *30*, 31
Olive-Cheese Balls, 14, *15*
Oven Caramel Corn, 36, *37*
Sausage Cheese Balls, *16*, 17
Savory Stuffed Mushrooms, *20*, 21
Smoked Salmon and Dill Canapés, 28, *29*

Apple(s)
-Grapefruit Salad, 148, *149*
Oven Pancake, *112*, 113
Waldorf Salad, *146*, 147

Applesauce Doughnuts, *122*, 123

B

Bacon
-Cheddar Deviled Eggs, 19
Cheese Sandwich Loaf, 96, *97*
Hot German Potato Salad, 160, *161*
Seven-Layer Salad, *150*, 151

Baked Alaska Cupcakes, 188–89, *189*

Banana(s)
-Chocolate Cream Pie, 207
Cream Pie, 206–7, *207*
Foster, 216
Hummingbird Upside-Down Poke Bundt Cake, 226, *227*

Bars, Date, 204, *205*

Bean(s)
Confetti Pot Roast, 81
Three-, Casserole, *172*, 173

Beef
Fajitas, 78, *79*
Ground, –Noodle Casserole, Creamy, 70, *71*
Meatloaf, *76*, 77
Pigs in Blankets, 86, *87*
Pot Roast; variations, 80–81, *81*
Reuben Deviled Eggs, 19
Sauerbraten, Slow Cooker, *84*, 85
Stew, 82, *83*
Stroganoff, *72*, 73
Stuffed Peppers, 66, *67*
Swedish Meatballs, *68*, 69
Swiss Steak, 74, *75*
Texas Hash, 65
Three-Bean Casserole, *172*, 173

Biscuits
Buttermilk, 126
Stir 'n Roll, 126

Bisquick recipes
Cherry Swirl Coffee Cake, 110, *111*
French Crepes Suzette, 212, *213*
Party Waffles Royale, *62*, 63
Peach Cobbler, 222, *223*
Raspberry Peek-a-Boos, 118, *119*
Sausage Cheese Balls, *16*, 17
Velvet Crumb Cake, 182, *183*

Breads. *See also* **Rolls**
Anadama, *134*, 135
Apple Oven Pancake, *112*, 113
Applesauce Doughnuts, *122*, 123
Buttermilk Biscuits, 126
Cinnamon-Butter Buns, 127
Irish Soda, *140*, 141
Mixer Batter Buns, 127
Popovers, 132, *133*
Puffy Oven Pancake, 113
Pumpkin-Cranberry Pecan, with

Boozy Whipped Cream, 142, *143*
Raspberry Peek-a-Boos, 118, *119*
Sally Lunn, 136, *137*
Spoon, Fluffy, 139
Stir 'n Roll Biscuits, 126
Swedish Limpa Rye, 138
Sweet Muffins, 114

Broccoli
-Lemon Salad, Healthified, *158*, 159
Turkey Divan, 64

Buns
Cinnamon-Butter, 127
Mixer Batter, 127

Buttermilk Biscuits, 126

Butterscotch Cream Pie, 207

C

Cakes. *See also* **Coffee Cakes**
Baked Alaska Cupcakes, 188–89, *189*
Caramel Snickerdoodle, 178, *179*
Chocolate Cake Roll, 187
Gingerbread, 184, *185*
Hummingbird Upside-Down Poke Bundt, 226, *227*
Jelly Roll, 186, *187*
Lemon Chiffon, 190, *191*
Lemon Curd Jelly Roll, 187
Starlight Yellow, *180*, 181
Velvet Crumb, 182, *183*
Whipped Cream Jelly Roll, 187

Canapés, Smoked Salmon and Dill, 28, *29*

Candies
Divinity, 203
White Ting-a-Lings, 217

Cantonese Chicken Chop Suey, *106*, 107

Caramel Corn, Nutty, 36, *37*

Caramel Corn, Oven, 36, *37*

Caramel Snickerdoodle Cake, 178, *179*

Caribbean Chicken Kabobs, 60, *61*

Carrot(s)
Beef Stew, 82, *83*

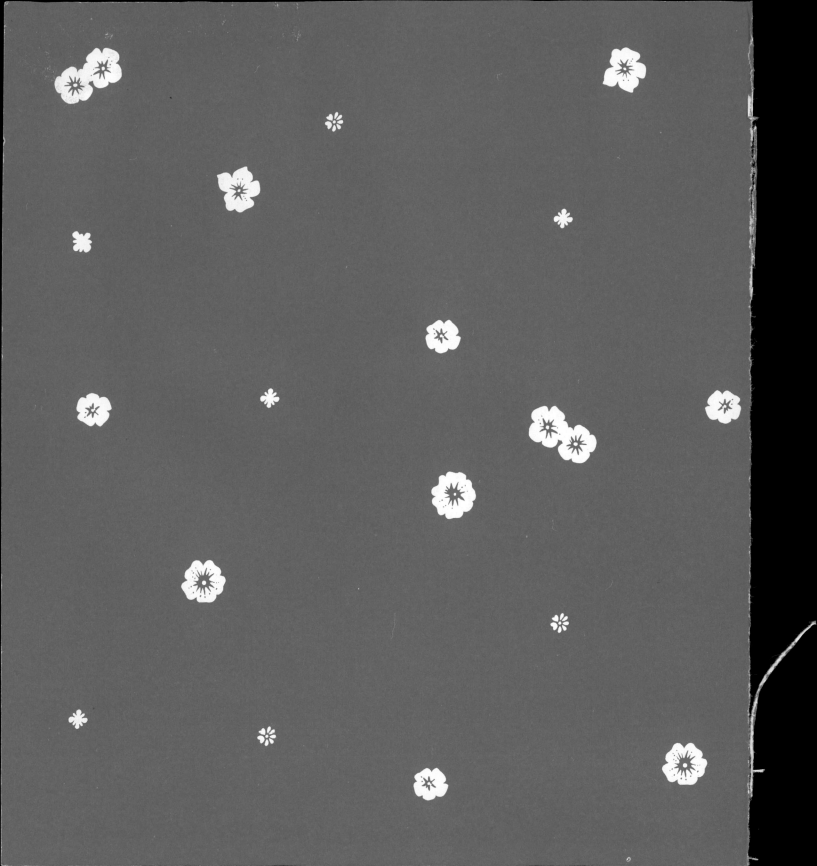